Editor Lesley Firth
Design Peter Benoist
Picture Research Christine Vincent
Production Rosemary Bishop
Illustrations Hayward Associates
                 Tony Payne
                 John Shackell
Maps Matthews and Taylor Associates
Consultant Dudley Ankerson

Photographic sources Key to positions
of illustrations: *(T)* top, *(C)* centre, *(B)*
bottom, *(L)* left, *(R)* right.
A.G.E. ilustración: *10(B)*, *31(BR)*,
35(T), *50(B)*, *53(B)*. Associated Press:
27(BR). The Bettmann Archive: *35(BR)*,
36-7(B), *37(BR)*. Bodleian Library:
8(L). British Museum: *33(TL)*. Camera
Press: *12(BL)*, *13(BR)*, *30(TL)*, *39(TR)*,
49(TL), *50(T)*, *52(CL)*, *52(TR)*:
photo John Gutmann Pix. M. Casasola:
37(TL), *37(TR)*. Cement and Concrete
Association: *49(TR)*. Culver Pictures:
36(TL), *36(BL)*, *37(CR)*. FAO: *51(BR)*.
Robert Harding Associates: (All photos
by Robert Cundy except where stated.)
15(BL): photo Sybil Sassoon. *16(BR)*,
17(BR), *19(BR)*: photo John Gardy.
21(BR), *24(BL)*, *28(TL)*, *39(BR)*,
43(TL), *47(B)*, *51(CL)*, *52(BL)*,
53(TL). Leo Hetzel: *29(TR)*, *52(TL)*.
Keystone: *33(CL)*, *50(CR)*. Mexican
Government Tourist Department:
40(TL), *46(BL)*, *51(TL)*. Dennis
Moore: *9(BR)*, *10(T)*, *11(BL)*,
11(BR), *14(TR)*, *15(TL)*, *15(TR)*,
15(CL), *17(TL)*, *18(BR)*, *19(TR)*,
20(TL), *21(TL)*, *21(TR)*, *22(TL)*,
23(TL), *24(TL)*, *24(TR)*, *24(BR)*,
27(TR), *28(BL)*, *28-9(B)*, *29(CR)*,
29(BR), *31(TL)*, *40(BL)*, *40(R)*,
41(BR), *42(BR)*, *43(B)*, *44(T)*,
44(BR), *45(BL)*, *48(B)*, *49(BL)*,
53(TR). National Film Archive: *19(TL)*.
Spectrum: *45(TR)*. Picturepoint:
12(BR), *19(BL)*, *25(TL)*, *34(B)*. Paul
Popper: *12(TL)*. Productions TéléVision
Rencontre: *9(TL)*, *30(TR)*. SEF:
30(BL), *43(TR)*, *45(TL)*, *45(CB)*.
Ronald Sheridan: *45(BR)*. ZEFA:
9(BL), *15(BR)*, *16(T)*, *17(TR)*,
17(BL), *21(BL)*, *23(C)*, *25(CT)*,
25(BL), *26(TC)*, *26(BL)*, *27(TL)*,
27(BL), *31(BL)*, *33(TR)*, *38(TL)*,
38(BL), *39(TL)*, *39(CL)*, *39(BL)*,
41(BL), *42(TL)*, *42(C)*, *42(BL)*,
46(T), *46(BR)*, *48(T)*, *49(BR)*.

First published 1976
Reprinted 1979
Macdonald Educational Ltd.
Holywell House, Worship Street
London EC2A 2EN

© Macdonald Educational Ltd. 1976

ISBN 0 356 05453 5 (cased edition)
ISBN 0 356 06528 6 (limp edition)

Made and printed by
Morrison & Gibb Limited
Edinburgh, Scotland

Colour reproduction by
Fotomecanica Iberico, Madrid

Endpaper: A majestic Toltec temple at
the archaeological site of Chichén Itzá in
Yucatan.

Page Six: Aztec musicians at a festival.

Mexico

the land and its people

John Howard

Macdonald Educational

Contents

Who are the Mexicans?

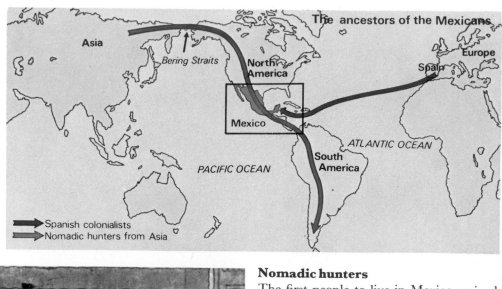

The ancestors of the Mexicans

→ Spanish colonialists
→ Nomadic hunters from Asia

▶ Before the arrival of the Spaniards in 1517, Europe was ignorant of the existence of Indian civilizations which had flourished for thousands of years in the Americas.

▼ Whilst searching for a place on which to found Tenochtitlán, the Aztecs saw an eagle devouring a snake on a cactus branch and took it as a sign from the gods. The emblem appears today on the Mexican flag.

Nomadic hunters

The first people to live in Mexico arrived about 20,000 years ago. They were nomadic hunters who crossed the Bering Straits from Asia during the Ice Age, when the continents were still connected. Many Mexican Indians today still have the Oriental features of their remote ancestors.

By about 5000 B.C. the first settlers in the valleys and coastal plains began to cultivate maize, beans, and pumpkins. The earliest civilizations developed in the centre of Mexico about 1800 B.C. and many technical and artistic skills then emerged.

Different tribes travelled across the country, and trade in food and craftwares began. The Olmecs, notable for their gigantic carved stone heads, settled near Vera Cruz about 1500 B.C. and strongly influenced the spread of civilization.

Indian and Spanish empires

Other Indian civilizations which began their cultures about this time were those of the Maya in Yucatan and the southeast, Zapotecs around Oaxaca, and the magnificent city-state of Teotihuacán on the central plateau. For hundreds of years empires and dynasties rose and fell, until the warlike Aztecs founded their capital Tenochtitlán in 1325 A.D. on the site of modern Mexico City.

Hernán Cortés landed at Vera Cruz on April 21st 1519, and after many fierce struggles captured Tenochtitlán and razed it to the ground. The last Aztec rulers, Moctezuma and Cuauhtémoc, were killed and their empire was destroyed. The Spaniards governed Mexico until the War of Independence freed the country in 1821.

The Mexican population today is formed of a still incomplete mixture of Indians and Spaniards.

◀ A giant stone head, carved by the Olmecs. The Olmecs were one of the earliest cultural groups of ancient times. They worshipped jaguar, snake and bird deities which demanded human sacrifices to ensure fertility. The Olmecs were a relatively highly advanced society. They developed astronomy and mathematics, and were potters and sculptors of genius.

The Mexicans today

Mexican Indians   Spaniards

▲ Most modern Mexicans are of mixed Spanish and Indian blood and are known as *mestizos*. The proportion of pure blood Indians is steadily declining.

◀ The Plaza of the Three Cultures in Mexico City. A new housing project in the old part of Mexico City included a site which had both the Aztec ruins of Tlatelolco and the beautiful Spanish Colonial Church of Santiago. The architect Mario Pani had the new Foreign Ministry built in the same ancient plaza. By this imaginative plan he preserved together three distinctive cultural landmarks.

9

A land of many faces

An extraordinary landscape

The vast horn shape of Mexico curves down from the United States border to the Central American countries of Guatemala and Belize. Its shores are washed by the blue waters of the Pacific, the Caribbean, and the Gulf of Mexico, whence flows the Gulf Stream.

Mexico is a land of snowcapped mountains and volcanoes, high plateaux, and tropical rain forests. Arid deserts contrast with placid lakes and green plantations. Its coastline and land borders extend over 14,000 kilometres (8,700 miles), enclosing a fascinating country six times the size of the British Isles.

Highest of all the snowy mountain peaks is the perfect cone of Orizaba, worshipped by the ancient Indians as the "Mountain of the Star". Rising above the Valley of Mexico is Ixtaccíhuatl ("The Sleeping Woman"). Watching over her nearby is her sentinel Popocatépetl ("The Smoking Mountain"). Their white mantles are a familiar sight to the millions of people living in Mexico City.

Deserts and jungles

Most of the desert country is in the north and west, but hundreds of thousands of acres of parched wastelands have been transformed into green and highly productive irrigation zones. By contrast the Gulf coast and humid jungles of Tabasco are drenched by torrential rains and battered by fierce hurricanes. Yucatan is uniquely different, a flat limestone peninsula which for thousands of years has been the home of the Maya Indians. Vast henequen plantations produce sisal hemp for making many of the world's ropes.

The sun shines brilliantly all over Mexico, but the temperature depends very much on the altitude. The central plateaux, known as the "altiplano", have a benign climate due to an average height of over 2,000 metres (6,500 ft). The concentration of population in this favoured region reflects the enjoyment of warm days and cool nights by more than thirty million Mexicans.

▲ When the volcano Popocatépetl rumbles and smokes, the Indians say he is mourning for his dead sweetheart, the dormant volcano Ixtaccíhuatl. An old legend relates how they were originally a Chichimeca prince and a Toltec princess forbidden to marry. The princess died of a broken heart.

▼ Guadalajara is the second largest city of Mexico and retains much of its old colonial atmosphere. It is famous for its *mariachi* music, animated street life, and enormous Libertad market. The climate is warm. Its Tlaquepaque district is one of Mexico's best centres for pottery and glass.

Mexico-a land of contrasts

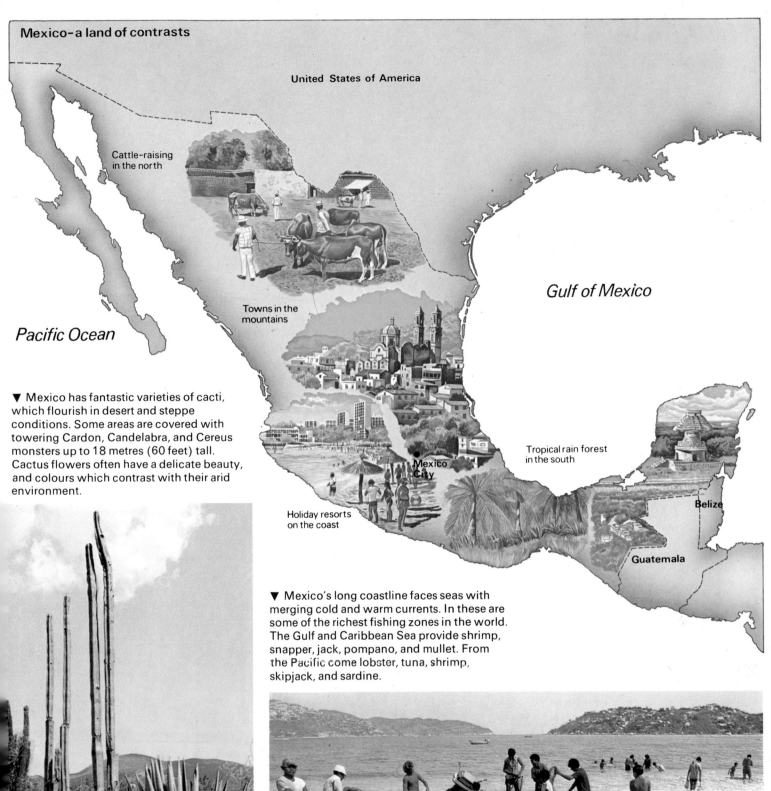

United States of America

Pacific Ocean

Cattle-raising
in the north

Towns in the
mountains

Gulf of Mexico

Mexico
City

Holiday resorts
on the coast

Tropical rain forest
in the south

Belize

Guatemala

▼ Mexico has fantastic varieties of cacti,
which flourish in desert and steppe
conditions. Some areas are covered with
towering Cardon, Candelabra, and Cereus
monsters up to 18 metres (60 feet) tall.
Cactus flowers often have a delicate beauty,
and colours which contrast with their arid
environment.

▼ Mexico's long coastline faces seas with
merging cold and warm currents. In these are
some of the richest fishing zones in the world.
The Gulf and Caribbean Sea provide shrimp,
snapper, jack, pompano, and mullet. From
the Pacific come lobster, tuna, shrimp,
skipjack, and sardine.

The Mexican character

▲ On the Day of the Dead (All Saints Day) Mexicans go to the cemeteries to eat, drink, and re-unite with departed relatives and friends. This small boy and girl wait for their brother's soul to join them.

▼ The Epiphany is Three Kings Day in Mexico, when presents are given instead of on Christmas Day. It is a time for family reunions. This Mexican family is being photographed with the Three Kings.

The Indian and Spanish heritage

The typical Mexican has a dual character. He or she inherits Indian stoicism, patience, fatalism, and silence, together with the pride, arrogance, and generosity of the Spaniard.

Courtesy is natural to both races, and no people are more graceful and polite than the Mexicans. Visitors are charmed by the friendly, genial welcome they meet everywhere. Nothing is too much trouble to please a guest, and the kindness and hospitality can be overwhelming.

Mexicans are proud of their long, eventful and historic heritage, and archaeologists are constantly making further discoveries, adding to their knowledge of a brilliant past.

The Mexicans are a dignified people. The poorest somehow manage to appear neat and clean on fiesta days, and children are proudly displayed in spotless if oft-mended clothes. The national characteristic of gracious good manners gives to the humblest Mexican the style of a grandee.

A contempt for death

All Saints Day is known as the Day of the Dead in Mexico. It is a feast day on which families go to the cemeteries to have parties. Food and drinks are offered to the departed relatives. Bakers sell specially made "death bread" decorated with skulls of icing, and sugar coffins, which are eagerly eaten in large quantities amidst the graves.

Young men commonly demonstrate their *machismo*—a kind of boastful manly pride—in the thick traffic roaring down city avenues. Darting into the path of hurtling cars, they make "passes" like those of bullfighters, defying drivers to run them down and usually escape violent death only by an inch or two. Others, at Acapulco, make hair raising dives from a very high rocky cliff, plunging into a narrow crevice just as a surging wave thunders in for barely enough depth of water.

Machismo tends to make some Mexicans more prone to violence. Mild disputes may very quickly erupt into angry struggles. Insults, real or imagined, can lead to the use of guns and knives. Mexico's very high murder rate is undoubtedly a result of this acceptance of blood and death as part of life.

Time is different in Mexico

Mexicans are a hard working people, quite unlike the popular image of idlers dozing in the sun under their broad sombreros. Long hours in fields, offices, shops, factories, and building sites, leave little time for long siestas in the afternoons.

But even for the most up-to-date Mexicans, time has not quite the same meaning as it has for us. The plumber who says "Eleven o'clock tomorrow morning without fail" will often turn up on time a week or a month later. *Mañana* means tomorrow, but in Mexico it can really be just another day.

▲ No Mexican plaza seems to be complete without a balloon seller. The plaza is the focus of social life. The evening *paseo*, when everyone strolls round, the boys in one direction, and the girls in the opposite, is a traditional Spanish custom. Girls are still strictly controlled by parents and not allowed to stay out late.

▲ The bear hug *abrazo* greeting gets its name from the Spanish word for arm—*brazo*. Obviously handshakes aren't friendly enough!

▲ Mexicans are inveterate gamblers. The State Lottery benefits from millions who hope their ticket will win them a fortune.

▼ Mariachis are groups of musicians who can be hired by a lover to play outside his girl friend's home just before dawn.

▲ Dicing with fast moving traffic is a very dangerous way of proving manliness *(machismo)*. It is not always successful!

▲ The countryman seen dozing under his sombrero is not the lazy idler of fiction. He has a long and hard day's work to do, and it is sensible to rest during the hottest hours of the day.

▶ On holidays Mexican men love to put on their freshly pressed clean clothes to gossip with friends in the shade.

Family life

Strong family ties

Mexicans have inherited the strong sense of family loyalty and close ties of both their Indian and Spanish ancestors. The mother is the heart of family gatherings, and uncles, aunts, cousins, and grandparents frequently meet to exchange gossip and news.

Families are usually large, and children are often absurdly doted upon. Old people are never abandoned, and there is no need for the old people's homes which sadly are so necessarily a part of the British scene.

The Church still wields immense influence, and there is little of the permissive way of life in Mexican middle class family society.

Social activities centre round numerous holidays, birthdays, Saints' days, weddings and festivals, when relatives and close friends fill the house to bursting point. Strangers and foreigners are rarely taken into a Mexican home. Mexicans prefer to entertain friends and business clients at favourite clubs and restaurants.

Early to bed

Lunch is traditionally the main meal of the day, when the family comes home to gather round the well laden table. Working days are hard and long, so father is usually only too glad to put up his feet when he gets home in the evening. Most families are content to stay quietly at home to watch the television. Those feeling more energetic may go out to their local cinema. Bedtime is usually early in agricultural areas. There are no long, light evenings in the tropics and darkness falls swiftly all the year round.

There is a very strong instinct for home ownership, and houses are often preferred to flats because of the intense love of the land. The affluent suburbs of large towns have many streets of neat homes, each with carefully tended gardens. Even blocks of flats are surrounded by lawns and flower beds. Mexican families have deep roots in the land for which so many fought and died in the Revolution.

▶ Mexican families are usually large. This family lives in Yucatan, where most of the people have a lot of Mayan blood. They are a handsome race of short stature and high intelligence. They are very proud of their ancient civilization.

An urban family timetable

7.00–7.30 am

8.00 am–1.00 pm

1.30 pm

3.00–6.00 pm

6.00–7.00 pm

7.00–10.00 pm

10.30–11.30 pm

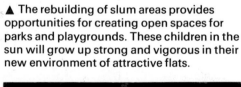

▲ The design of modern houses like this is influenced by the dry sunny climate. The spacious terrace is a favourite leisure time part of the home. Petrol is relatively cheap in Mexico so a large American type car is not extravagant.

▲ A poor village like this shows how much needs to be done to raise the living standards in many rural areas. As industrial production continues to grow, many of these villagers will eventually be moved to districts where they can earn better wages.

▲ The rebuilding of slum areas provides opportunities for creating open spaces for parks and playgrounds. These children in the sun will grow up strong and vigorous in their new environment of attractive flats.

◄ The sound of maize being ground on stone *metates*, and the pat-a-pat of tortilla pan-cakes being shaped by hand, have been heard for thousands of years. Now the machine age is catching up on this traditional task of the Mexican housewife and saves her much time and energy.

▲ Despite poverty, and lack of tap water in many homes, Mexicans are notably clean people. Women and children sometimes wash their clothes and put them on again at once so that they quickly dry on their bodies in the hot sunshine. These women enjoy an opportunity for light hearted gossip.

A religious society

▲ The Guadalupe Shrine is the holiest in Mexico. Its Virgin is venerated by the Mexicans so much that they crawl on their knees across the great concourse to worship at her miraculously painted image.

▶ All the Mexican love of dressing up and ritual parades is shown in this picture of Saints being carried on processional floats. To many Mexicans the richly garbed statues have a real and living compassion for the faithful. Men who carry the heavy images are extremely proud of the privilege.

Pagan gods

Religious beliefs have been a fundamental part of Mexican culture for thousands of years. Christianity began with the Spanish Conquest, and was built on a pagan base so that the Indians were able to accept the new devotion at their old familiar shrines. Many of the early churches were founded on sites where the ancient Indian gods had been worshipped, and the wiser Christian friars were able to convert the natives by allowing the new rites to continue in place of the old.

Pre-Conquest religious cults varied with the different Indian groups living throughout the vastness of Mexico. They began with gods of elemental and peaceful aspect, but as the tribes became more aggressive, and warriors ranked with priests, religion became linked with war.

The old Rain God, Tlaloc, and the God of Wisdom, Quetzalcóatl, were then joined by bloodthirsty deities demanding more and more sacrifices for their maintenance. The reeking temples of the Aztecs were piled high with corpses and skulls. Hearts were torn out of living bodies with obsidian blades, and were sometimes devoured by the blood spattered priests to appease the God of War, Huitzilopochtli. Thousands of victims were sometimes sacrificed in a single day, but fortunately not all the Indian tribes were addicted to such grisly rites, as their own gods never became so malignant.

Fiestas and churches

The Spanish word *fiesta* really has the same meaning as our feast-day. Both are religious in origin. In Mexico, local Saints and Virgins are worshipped and their anniversaries celebrated with much the same ritual as was used in ancient times. Some of these have become nationally famous and attract throngs of many thousands of devout pilgrims from all over the country.

The Virgin of Guadalupe, as Patroness of the Republic, has the place of honour in her Sanctuary in Mexico City. As in Spain, Holy Week is a time of devout religious spirit, with solemn processions and Passion plays culminating on Easter Day with joyful explosions of fireworks.

Many of the earlier churches clearly show how their Indian builders and craftsmen adapted their skills, merging the pagan with the new Christian religion. Richly decorated ornamental work, so beloved by the Indians, included cunningly carved pagan figures and symbols amongst the gilded and painted angels and cherubs.

▲ Imaginatively created home shrines are often found amongst Mexican Catholics. Many are still devoted to their religion despite State suppression of the Church's power.

► This Nativity play is being performed in the Shrine of the Virgin of the Remedies, Patroness of the Spaniards, to whom prayers are offered for rain and cures for sickness. A Conquistador brought her image from Spain.

◄ The close personal relationship between deeply religious people and the images which they cherish most, is shown by this mother and child kissing a figure of Christ. He is especially loved by young children.

▼ Passion plays are enacted in many towns and villages during Holy Week. The art and skill with which the various costumes are made reflect the national genius for handicrafts, and the enthusiasm of the people.

Leisure and pleasure

▼ The Mexican *charros* were the origin of American cowboys. They used to look after the cattle on the vast haciendas. Their distinctive, silver studded costumes are now a feature of modern rodeos with thrilling horsemanship.

Happiness is noisy!

Ask a Mexican what he enjoys most and he will beam with delight as he replies "Eating and drinking!" Eating out in family groups and parties of friends is the favourite way of celebrating weekends and fiesta days. Restaurants and picnic grounds are filled with noisy throngs having the time of their lives. The men jovially thump each others backs in the affectionate hugs of welcome they call *abrazos*, from the Spanish word for arm.

The cinema is still tremendously popular. and Mexico has had its own substantial film making industry for decades. Some of the leading movie stars such as Dolores del Río, María Félix, Pedro Armendariz, and Jorge Negrete achieved international fame. The great comedian Marío Moreno, known as "Cantinflas", is the Charlie Chaplin of the Spanish and Latin American screen.

Many American films, especially Westerns, are made in Mexico, and the northern city of Durango became a second home for John Wayne. Luis Buñuel has enriched the whole world of the cinema with his brilliant and controversial films, notably his grim and tragic *Los Olvidados* (*The Lost Ones*).

The magnet of television

Television has made phenomenal progress in recent years, strongly influenced by vast technical resources and production facilities

▶ Puppet or marionette shows were brought to Mexico by the Spaniards, and the Indians quickly mastered this difficult and fascinating art. Their craftsmanship produces remarkably life-like figures to entertain adults and children in parks and theatres.

brought in by the neighbouring USA. TV aerials sprout thickly over the roofs of even the poorest suburbs. Bars and cafes have sets for their customers, and become crammed with enthusiasts when important football matches and bullfights are being shown.

The quality of Mexican TV is very variable and there is far too much advertising time. But an interesting exception is the channel of programmes devoted entirely to intellectually stimulating lectures, debates, and lessons of many kinds.

The theatre has comparatively little popular support, but musical concerts, revues, and above all, the famous folklore ballet, play to full houses.

Sunny days for fiestas

The benign climate enables everyone to take advantage of the many fiesta days to head for the beaches, parks, and woodlands to swim, get a tan, or doze in the shade. With over 9,650 kilometres (6,000 miles) of coastline, Mexico has plenty of beaches and warm blue seas.

Many towns have bandstands in the central plazas, and the sound of marimba and brass bands draws appreciative crowds. Night clubs and discotheques are always crammed with couples showing the Mexican flair for rhythmic music and dancing.

◀ Marío Moreno, known as "Cantinflas", was a top film star in Mexico for many years. His comedy genius made him the Charlie Chaplin of the Spanish speaking world. He won fame in America and Britain when he played Passepartout, David Niven's companion in the film *Round the World in Eighty Days*.

▲ The reliably dry, sunny weather of most of Mexico makes a picnic an enjoyable outing which can be planned weeks ahead. There is every kind of scenery to be found in this huge country, and there are National Parks in which the environment and wild life are protected and preserved. Let's hope a wild jaguar did not disturb this happy party !

▲ News-stands show a dual Spanish-American influence. This collection of children's magazines has many American stories translated into Spanish. There are innumerable women's journals similar in style to those read in Spain. Leading daily newspapers like *Excelsior* are of high quality.

◀ There is much less night life in Mexico than one might expect. It flourishes only in the largest cities and the most popular tourist resorts like Acapulco. This is an elegant Spanish club in Mexico City with American tourists watching the cabaret.

Educational progress

▼ Improvements in the schooling and welfare of young children are now producing bright and healthy future citizens just like these. Importance is attached to moulding their characters and bodies as well as to their first lessons.

Problems and policies

Mexico's educational achievements during the last decade have been amongst the most remarkable of any country in the world. Some of the problems to be overcome have included a rapidly increasing population, centuries of a very high rate of illiteracy, and dozens of complex Indian languages.

The Government has provided substantial financial support for a sustained improvement in education at all levels, designed to make it more compatible with the country's economic development process. High priority is given to the reform of primary and basic secondary education on the one hand, and promotion of scientific and technical resources on the other.

The fundamental aim of Mexico's educational policy is to provide every child with primary schooling. More and more children finishing their primary classes are being enabled to enter secondary schools, and higher educational facilities for secondary students are also expanding.

Fostering of adult and postgraduate studies, development of better co-operation between universities and technological institutions, and industry and research, are also important parts of the educational programme.

Schools and universities

The Ministry of Public Education is the Federal Government agency responsible for educational and cultural affairs. There are now more than 50,000 schools and training centres. Four-fifths of all schools are devoted to primary education. Secondary schools account for less than a tenth of the total, whilst there are more than 300 university schools and faculties and professional level institutes. The National Autonomous University and the National Polytechnic Institute together have more than fifty per cent of the students receiving higher education.

The National University is the oldest on the American continent, founded by Charles V of Spain in 1551. Its vast campus, with more than 100,000 students, has some of the most brilliantly designed and colourful modern buildings in the world.

Growth of educational budget

The Ministry's budget is by a large margin the highest of any Government department and has an annual growth of about twelve per cent. It is responsible for providing all but about eleven per cent of educational facilities, the remainder being supported by private resources.

Primary school ages are between six and 14, secondary 15 to 19, and the higher institutes have students aged from 19 to 24. The trend during the most recent years has been for proportionately more money to be provided for secondary and university facilities.

Nursery schools are being provided in the larger towns. The rate of population increase has, however, made it difficult for the Ministry to maintain educational standards. About one third of the population is still classified as illiterate.

The Mexican system of education

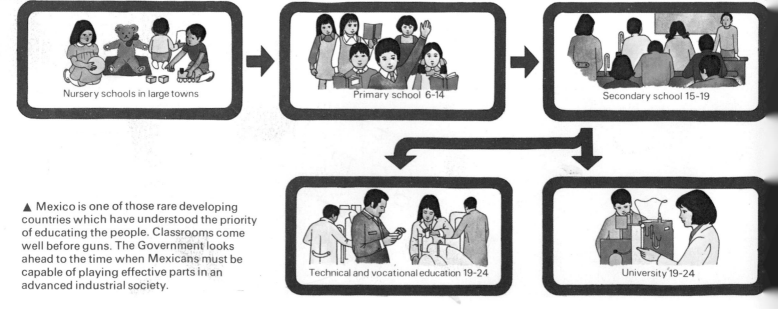

Nursery schools in large towns

Primary school 6-14

Secondary school 15-19

Technical and vocational education 19-24

University 19-24

▲ Mexico is one of those rare developing countries which have understood the priority of educating the people. Classrooms come well before guns. The Government looks ahead to the time when Mexicans must be capable of playing effective parts in an advanced industrial society.

▼ The instinct for handicraft work is highly developed in Mexico. Open air schools, like this one in the capital's Chapultepec Park, have many enthusiastic students. This girl is learning woodwork. With the active encouragement of the State she should develop her skill to a professional and well paid standard.

▲ Well designed, modern schools like this make lessons a pleasure for these young pupils. The Education Ministry controls funds to continue development of an ideal given birth when most Mexicans were utterly impoverished and illiterate.

▼ The National University now has over 100,000 students, and its vast campus and superb modern buildings are no longer large enough. Plans for extensions will surely inspire Mexico's architects and artists to create an even greater seat of learning.

▲ The Tarahumara Indians live in northern Mexico and are famous as the fastest and most enduring runners of all the American peoples. They chase and run down stags as a sport, and then set them free as they are sacred animals. They are a poor but proud and independent people who often live in caves on a high plateau. This Jesuit missionary school cares for the children of a small Tarahumara village, which is cold in winter and scorching hot in summer. Some remote missions, founded by friars in the early years after the Conquest, still continue the work begun by those great and good men over 400 years ago. There can be no better teachers for the Indians.

Mexico's unique food and drinks

▲ The patio of this converted old Colonial palace is a pleasant place in which to eat delicious Mexican food in warm sunshine and elegant surroundings.

Traditional cooking

It is surprisingly difficult to find Mexican restaurants in which traditional native food is prepared and served. Most tourists are Americans who, like the British, are apt to prefer bland tasting meals. So to avoid the tame visitors' menus some exploration may be necessary. This is well worth the effort!

Eating Mexican style is an adventure and a delight. The highly piquant and pungent flavours have been enjoyed almost unchanged for centuries. Maize and beans have been basic ingredients since they were first cultivated in Mexico thousands of years ago. The dozens of varieties of chilli peppers add their uniquely fiery flavour and are an important source of vitamins.

Regional variations

Many Mexican States have their own regional specialities and styles of cooking. Puebla is the home of *Mole Poblana*, the national favourite, a noble dish of turkey simmered slowly with many spices, chocolate, chillies, and nuts. *Carne Asada*, marinated strips of beef grilled with a peppery avocado, tomato, and garlic sauce, is popular in the northern cattle raising states.

Bitter oranges are used for flavouring in Yucatan, where meat and fish are cooked wrapped in banana leaves. Seafood is at its best on the Gulf coast, where restaurants in Vera Cruz serve succulent dishes of red snapper, snook, bass, kingfish, and jumbo sized shrimps.

Fruits and vegetables of every kind grow abundantly in Mexico's varied climate. Melons, tomatoes and strawberries are now valuable export crops. The country is one of the leading producers of high quality coffee, and its chocolate was first grown by Indians many hundreds of years ago.

Drinks for all tastes

Mexico's lager type beers are popular. Cactus plantations produce a mildly alcoholic beverage called *pulque* which is drunk mostly by the poorer folk. *Tequila* and *mescal* are two highly potent spirits distilled from a liquid extracted from cactus plants. They are traditionally drunk with salt and freshly squeezed limes.

Make yourself a Mexican meal

GUACAMOLE
2 large, ripe avocados
1 tablespoon finely chopped onion
2 teaspoons finely chopped tinned chilli
1 tomato, peeled and chopped
1 tablespoon chopped fresh coriander
salt and pepper to taste

Peel the avocados and remove the stones. Mash the avocados into a pulp with a fork in a bowl. Then mix in the other ingredients carefully. Cover the guacamole with foil and place in a refrigerator until it is ready to be used. Serve it as a dip, or with salad at the start of your meal.

PICADILLO
2 lbs minced beef
1 onion, chopped
1 clove garlic, chopped
3 tomatoes, peeled and chopped
2 cooking apples, peeled, cored and chopped
3 tinned chillies, washed and finely sliced
2 oz raisins
12 stuffed olives, sliced across
¼ teaspoon ground cinnamon
¼ teaspoon ground cloves
2 oz blanched, sliced almonds

3 tablespoons olive oil
salt and pepper to taste

Heat 2 tablespoons of olive oil in a heavy pan. Add the minced beef and stir until it is browned all over. Then add the onion and garlic and cook for a few minutes before adding all the other ingredients, except the almonds. Simmer for 30 minutes. In the meantime, heat the rest of the olive oil in a frying pan and add the almonds. Fry for a few minutes until they are golden. Add the almonds to the picadillo when it is cooked. Serve with rice.

CALABAZA ENMIELADA
3 lb piece of pumpkin (or marrow) cut into six pieces
1 lb brown sugar
6 tablespoons of water
¼ pint whipped cream

Remove the seeds from the pumpkin or marrow. Put the water in a shallow ovenproof dish and arrange the pieces of pumpkin in it. Sprinkle with the sugar and bring to the boil. Cover the dish and simmer for an hour, basting with the syrupy liquid every 15 minutes. When tender, allow to cool. Arrange the pumpkin in dishes, pour the syrup over them, and top with whipped cream.

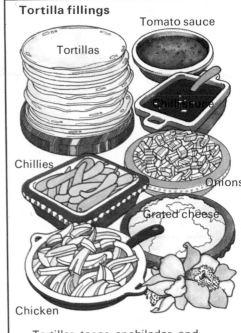

Tortilla fillings

Tomato sauce

Tortillas

Chilli sauce

Chillies

Onions

Grated cheese

Chicken

▲ Fruit grows so abundantly in Mexico that freshly squeezed juices are cheap and popular. How much better they taste than factory-made, bottled soft drinks! Orange juice is the regular breakfast starter in many homes, and the warm weather keeps the squeezers busy and the customers happy.

Tortillas, tacos, enchiladas, and tamales are all made from maize and wheat flour. They are stuffed with variations of fillings based on those shown above. Tamales are steamed inside wrappers of maize or banana leaves, whilst the other three kinds of pancake are fried or baked.

Regional dishes

◄ Maguey agave plantations are common in the dry central plateau. The liquid tapped from their hearts is made into the mildly alcoholic beverage called *pulque*.

▼ Street stalls like this are found in the poorer suburbs and in villages. Practically everything, including meat, is bought and sold on a day to day basis by the owner. Customers cannot afford to store food, so it is all sold freshly picked or killed.

▲ Regarded as *the* national dish of Mexico, Mole Poblana's turkey is cooked with a sauce of over 30 ingredients, including chocolate.

▲ The warm seas surrounding Yucatan teem with exotic fish. These are cooked with savoury spices in Creole style.

23

Shops and markets

▲ Modern supermarkets like these are American in style, and are more attractive and efficient than most British stores. Customers are mostly middle class car-owning families who are able to afford the better quality merchandise and service.

▲ The revolution changed many things in Mexico but the age-old instinct for bartering still strongly survives. Mexican women enjoy running market stalls and shops, and the children quickly develop trading ability and a love of independence.

Supermarkets galore

Perhaps unexpectedly in a country where so many of the traditional family owned little shops still thrive, supermarkets are now to be seen everywhere.

A Government sponsored company runs an extensive chain of popular priced shops created to improve the living standards of the poorer people. It also has mobile shops travelling through remote rural areas.

Fascinating Indian markets

The animated native markets continue their colourful displays, even in the midst of busy towns. Guadalajara's vast Libertad market retains its Indian style and character despite being under the cover of a modern concrete building. The Friday market of the cold highland city of Toluca is still a Mecca for thousands of Mexicans and tourists alike.

Fascinating and sometimes macabre stalls sell strange looking herbs and medicinal plants, including the peyote which causes hallucinations.

An unusual and often rewarding place for shopping in Mexico City is Monte de Piedad, the National Pawnshop. It is owned by the State, and occupies an old palace near the Cathedral. Fine jewels, heirlooms, antique furniture, and Old Master paintings can sometimes be bought by an early and discerning visitor.

▲ Most herbs and spices sold in Mexican markets are used in cooking. Others are for curing fevers, healing wounds, or even warding off evil spirits. Medical researchers have long been interested in hallucinogenic plants in Mexico such as peyote.

◄ Although many of the old style markets are now under cover, they retain their function of selling fresh food from individually owned stalls. Most Mexicans really enjoy shopping here, but the rich usually send their more than willing servants.

▼ Butchers' stalls like these have a red flag hanging outside on the days when they have freshly slaughtered meat. In poor villages without refrigeration meat must be sold quickly to avoid spoiling in the hot climate.

Handicrafts sold in Mexican markets

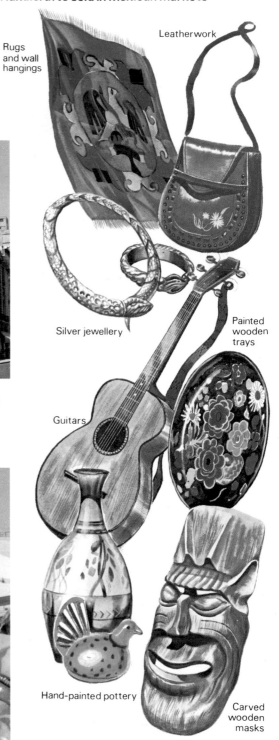

Rugs and wall hangings

Leatherwork

Silver jewellery

Painted wooden trays

Guitars

Hand-painted pottery

Carved wooden masks

▲ Once a nobleman's palace, this beautiful building is entirely covered with coloured tiles. It is now a famous gift shop with a popular restaurant in its patio.

▲ Shopping in Mexico is probably more fun and more rewarding than in any other country. Craftsmen produce a great variety of articles of charm and beauty. You can often watch the craftsmen at work.

◄ Toluca's Friday market is noted for native handicrafts like this pottery. Bought by Mexicans for use at home, and by tourists as souvenirs, craftware like this is made in scores of villages in the region.

25

Sport

▲ The Spaniards brought bullfighting to Mexico when they established their immense cattle ranches in the north.

◄ Played with a *cesta* basket strapped to the forearm, pelota is the fastest ball game of all. Only a few top ranking professional players can maintain their lightning reflexes after they are about 30 years old.

▼ The ease with which cockfights can be staged anywhere, in or out of doors, makes them very popular. Betting is fast and furious as the highly trained birds fight, cheered on by eager supporters.

Bullfights and charros

Sports enthusiasts find plenty of action in Mexico, where the climate permits year round play. Mexico was host to the Olympic Games in 1968 and the World Soccer Championship in 1970.

Mexico, like Spain, is a country of horsemanship and bullfighting. But although the Plaza in Mexico City is the world's largest bullring, the spectacle is somewhat less popular than in Spain.

Horses, however, are a real passion. The brilliant exhibitions of riding, in rodeos called *charreadas*, are watched with delight by cheering crowds. Both sexes wear the uniquely Mexican *charro* costumes, studded with gold and silver, and topped by massive sombreros with specially shaped brims. Ranches in many parts of the country provide healthy and energetic holidays over miles of scenic trails.

The fastest ball game

The ancient Basque game of *jai-alai*, also called *pelota*, is undoubtedly the fastest ball game in the world. The slower handball form of the game is played on small courts found all over the country. But the large cities have long three walled courts with spectator galleries where the top ranking professionals compete. The players have scoops of wicker called *cestas* strapped to their arms which catch the hard elastic ball and shoot it out at lightning speed against the walls. Betting on the games adds to the excitement of the yelling fans in the gallery.

The biggest spectator sport is undoubtedly soccer—*futbol* to the Mexicans. The huge Azteca Stadium in Mexico City seats over 100,000 enthusiasts, and there are leagues of clubs similar to those in Britain. Many leading European and South American teams play in international matches here.

Cockfights and boxing

Cockfighting is very popular. It is easy to stage anywhere and attracts large sums of money in the very keen and noisy betting as the highly trained birds struggle for supremacy.

Mexico has produced many world class boxing champions, especially in the lightweight divisions. Baseball draws avid fans to see star players from both Mexican and American league teams. Motor racing aficionados can see the world's fastest drivers in the International Grand Prix race in October.

◀ Warm Pacific Ocean rollers are ideal for surfers and acrobatic swimmers who enliven Acapulco's beaches by their daring skill. Acapulco is Mexico's most popular tourist resort.

▲ Basketball owes its popularity to the neighbouring USA, where it is a leading sport. It is an athletic game for youngsters of both sexes and is inexpensive to set up.

▲ The athlete Ron Clarke was given oxygen after the finish of the Olympic 10,000 metres final in Mexico, 1968. This shows the exhausting effects of high altitude. It takes many weeks to get used to the rarified atmosphere. Some athletes failed badly in the Olympic Games of 1968.

◀ The Azteca Stadium in Mexico City holds 100,000 soccer fans. Seen here is an international match between Mexico and Colombia.

Transport and communications

The rapid progress of recent years in communications and transport has helped to bring greater efficiency to the economy and integration of the country. Growth rate is impressive, Mexico now being third only to the USA and Canada in extension of paved highways, and its air and shipping services are well established internationally.

The Pan-American Highway runs over 3,200 kilometres (2,000 miles) through Mexico, and the road network extends well over 80,500 kilometres (50,000 miles). Remarkable feats of engineering in mountainous country and across deep canyons have marked a still-continuing progress.

Transport bottlenecks in Mexico City's metropolitan area have been eased by the construction of a collective system using both underground and surface trains capable of moving large masses of people quickly and safely across the sprawling capital.

Hundreds of airports

The local and international air services are being improved and extended. There are no less than 77 Mexican airlines in operation, the leading companies flying jets on international routes.

There are over 5,000 post offices, and mail processing is rapidly being automated. Satellite communications have been set up to integrate the national telecommunications network with those of the rest of the world.

▲ Airstrips are essential in mountain and forest country where there are no roads. This landing ground is in Chiapas, a tropical State which has many archaeological sites accessible only by air or by mule tracks. Pilots of these small planes develop great skill in tough conditions.

▼ Container trucks have to travel thousands of miles in blazing sunshine, so must be able to carry large loads insulated from the tropical heat. The well-engineered main roads of Mexico enable these monsters to travel safely at high average speeds over very long distances.

▲ Many buses serving minor country roads are worn out and frequently break down. They are often overloaded and are disastrous when their brakes fail on sharp mountain bends. Pigs, goats, and chickens are regular passengers on creaking vehicles with colourful names such as "The Five Wounds of Christ".

▲ Deep excavations for an underground rail system have revealed many remains of the Aztec capital Tenochtitlán, upon which Mexico City is built. Metro travellers can now view the art of their remote ancestors.

▶ Horses are a common form of transport in Mexico today. They were first introduced by the Spaniards when they conquered Mexico. The Indians were terrified of the horses at first and thought they were gods.

▼ The wide main highways and city avenues enable heavy traffic to proceed swiftly and smoothly. American and German cars dominate the fast growing automobile industry.

▼ In Mexico City some taxis are called *peseros* and have regular runs up and down the main avenues. They can be boarded anywhere on payment of a standard one peso fare, hence their name.

Ancient Mexico

This majestic Toltec temple called the Castillo is part of the enormous archaeological site of Chichén Itzá in Yucatan. It was built between 800 and 1200 AD.

▼ The painted walls of Bonampak, remote in the Chiapas jungles, were revealed by the dwindling band of Lacandon Indians, descendants of the Maya. These frescoes are masterpieces of the ancient world.

Mysterious stone heads

Long before the arrival of the Spaniards in 1519, a succession of Indian civilizations rose and fell, perhaps beginning about 1500 B.C. with the Olmecs. Their culture centred round La Venta, near modern Vera Cruz. They were pyramid builders notable for their delicate figurines and bowls shaped as animals and humans. Their enormous carved stone heads found in the jungles are still a mystery.

The Zapotecs settled in the warm valleys of Oaxaca, assimilating much of the culture of the Olmecs. Monte Albán became their principal centre. Excavations have revealed scores of elaborate tombs, plazas, an immense ball court, and many vast temples. Following a collapse of the Zapotec regime, the Mixtec people moved into the area and contributed their fine craftsmanship in jade, onyx, silver, and gold, and built the lovely religious centre of Mitla.

Mayan magnificence

The Maya inhabited the farspread territory covering Yucatan, southern Mexico, and part of Central America. Their formative period began about 1500 B.C. and the peak of their very advanced society lasted from about 400 A.D. to 900 A.D. They built many magnificent centres such as Palenque, Tikal, and Chichén Itzá, architectural and sculptural masterpieces. The Maya were skilled astronomers and developed a calendar system more accurate than our own.

In the great valley of Anáhuac the Mexica people founded fabulous Teotihuacán ("City of the Gods") where huge pyramids and temples line the majestic Avenue of the Dead.

The Toltecs, a race of builders and warriors, founded their great capital Tula in the ninth century. The glory of Tula is the now restored House of Tlahuizcalpante-cuhtli, ("Lord of the Dawn") and its mighty columns of Warriors of the Sun.

The last great Indian State was that of the Aztecs, who founded Tenochtitlán in 1325 A.D. on an island in Lake Texcoco. It grew rapidly over reclaimed ground as the capital of a vast empire. The Spaniards marvelled at the size and magnificence of what was perhaps then the largest city in the world, but did not hesitate to destroy it.

This Zapotec funerary urn came from a tomb in the great ceremonial centre, Monte Albán, near Oaxaca. The richly decorated figure bears the masks of an eagle and a jaguar, showing Olmec influence. It dates from about 300 AD. Magnificent treasures of gold and jade have been discovered here.

▲ This picture from a Mixtec codex (plural: codices) shows a priest piercing the nose of an official so he can wear his ceremonial jade bar of office plugged through his nose. Elaborately designed gold ornaments like earrings were also worn in this manner.

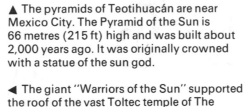

▲ The pyramids of Teotihuacán are near Mexico City. The Pyramid of the Sun is 66 metres (215 ft) high and was built about 2,000 years ago. It was originally crowned with a statue of the sun god.

◀ The giant "Warriors of the Sun" supported the roof of the vast Toltec temple of The House of the Lord of the Dawn at Tula. From here the legendary Quetzalcóatl, the plumed serpent god, ruled earth and sky.

▶ The Mixtecs recorded their history on exquisitely painted books called codices, made of long strips of beaten fibre paper folded zig-zag fashion. Few specimens of this form of pictographic writing survived the Conquest.

▼ This brilliantly coloured mural painting in the Municipal Palace of Mexico City is of ancient Tlaxcala. The people of Tlaxcala helped Cortés to defeat the Aztecs, and were the first to become Christians.

▲ A Mixtec chief called Eight Deer was involved in dynastic wars for control of an empire. He is shown capturing a nine year old relative, Four Wind, who because of his youth was spared the customary death under the sacrificial knife for the gods.

Spanish Conquest and Viceroyalty

Arrival at Tenochtitlán

Hernán Cortés landed near Vera Cruz on Good Friday, 1519, with a small force of 555 men and 16 horses. He led them through fever ridden jungles and icy mountain passes to the Aztec Empire's fabulous capital city Tenochtitlán.

The Emperor Moctezuma believed that the pale faced Spaniards were of divine origin, and received Cortés and his men as honoured visitors. The wily Cortés imprisoned the Emperor by a trick and became master of the city. But during his absence in Vera Cruz, his Lieutenant, Pedro de Alvarado, murdered some of the Aztec hostages. The people rose in a fury, but Cortés managed to get back to lead the Spaniards out of the besieged palace after Moctezuma was killed.

The last Aztec Emperor

The following year Cortés reformed his army and stormed Tenochtitlán. After weeks of desperate fighting, the valiant new Emperor Cuauhtémoc surrendered. The city was razed to the ground, and Cuauhtémoc was executed in 1524 after terrible tortures.

The Viceroyalty

As soon as the Spaniards established their rule over "New Spain", exploration, colonization, and exploitation of the country began. In 1535 the first Viceroy, Mendoza, arrived from Spain. All authority was vested in the Crown, and a Council was instituted to take responsibility for legislation. Spaniards born in Mexico, called Creoles, were never allowed any significant part in the government of the country.

Although the kings of Spain desired that the Indians should be protected from cruelty and exploitation, conditions for the natives were often harsh and many of them lived in poverty and servitude. Some of the earlier friars sent out from Spain worked to protect and teach the Indians, but the increasingly rich Church in Mexico became indifferent to their suffering.

Fatal epidemics

Imported European diseases such as smallpox decimated the population, and agricultural production fell. Fertile land was abandoned, leading to the creation of enormous estates called *haciendas* with a peonage system of labour which was really slavery.

The production of the mines assured the Spanish Treasury of a prodigious flow of silver and gold. Aristocratic mine owners lived in huge palaces and entertained on a princely scale.

At the end of the eighteenth century the Creole leaders of society in New Spain began to want a greater share in government. They bided their time for an opportunity to get rid of the Spanish masters and create a free Mexico.

▼ Hernán Cortés landed at Vera Cruz on April 21st, 1519 with a small force. Their long march to Tenochtitlán was joined by Totonac and Tlaxcalan Indians who were hostile to the Aztecs. Only after long sieges and heavy losses did the Spaniards conquer the city on August 13th, 1521.

The conquest of Mexico

ATLANTIC OCEAN
GULF OF MEXICO
CUBA
Villa Rica de la Vera Cruz
Tenochtitlán
Cholula Tlaxcala
Tabasco
YUCATAN PENINSULA
CARIBBEAN SEA

← Route of Cortés 1519

◄ Tenochtitlán was perhaps the largest city in the world at the height of its glory. The Spaniards were overwhelmed by the splendour of its huge temples, palaces, and unique floating gardens glittering in the centre of Lake Texcoco. A Spanish officer, Bernal Díaz later wrote an account of the Conquest, and said "Never had they ever seen such marvels"

◄ When Cortés first landed on the Mexican coast he received a gift of some native women, one of whom, called Malinche, became his interpreter. She accompanied him to Tenochtitlán and is pictured talking with Cortés to an Aztec ambassador.

▼ Morelia, capital of Michoacán State, is the most beautiful and best preserved of the large colonial cities of Mexico. It has a superb cathedral and many handsome old buildings of soft pink trachyte stone, like this convent with its dignified patio.

▲ Diego Rivera's murals represent the Spaniards as the cruel oppressors of gentle and innocent natives. Such naïvety does not obscure the genius of this great artist, as this picture shows.

► 1 The caste system of the colonial empire was headed by Spaniards born in Spain, with Creoles (Mexican born Spaniards without real power) ranking just below.
2. Marriages between Spaniards and *mestizos* of mixed blood produced children who could be accepted as being of middle caste, especially if they had pale skin.
3. Children of a pure blooded Indian father were always regarded as low caste even if the mother had Spanish blood.

Independence and the Republic

The Liberty Bell

On September 16th, 1810, Father Miguel Hidalgo, parish priest of the little town of Dolores, rang his church bell and shouted to wildly cheering people, "Viva Mexico! Death to the Spaniards!" Within a few days the rebels took many cities and controlled large areas of the country. After ferocious massacres and cruel retaliation by Royalist forces, Hidalgo was captured and executed.

Another priest, José María Morelos, joined the rebels and became their leader, proving to be an astute statesman and soldier. He presided over a Congress at Chilpancingo in 1813, affirming democratic government. Then he too was captured and put to death.

A young and unscrupulous Creole soldier, Agustín de Iturbide, then obtained the support of the rebels and triumphantly entered Mexico City in 1821. As Spain refused to recognize an independent Mexico, Iturbide had himself crowned as Emperor Agustín I. His profligate reign ended within a year, when he was forced to abdicate. A new Congress elected General Guadalupe Victoria as the first President of the Federal Republic in 1824.

Bankruptcy and reform

The poverty and unsettled state of the new republic was the principal cause of the long period of violent instability. Futile governments became involved in disastrous wars with Texas and the United States, and ceded vast territories to the Americans. Mexico became bankrupt.

Benito Juárez, a truly great figure in Mexico's history, became President in 1861. He crushed the brief French-backed reign of the Hapsburg Maximilian, and began the task of reconstructing the shattered country. Worn out by the struggle, he died in office in 1872.

In 1876, Porfirio Díaz seized power. The long dictatorship of Díaz restored order and progress, but the Indians and the poor were denied liberty and land, and the stage was set for the Revolution of 1910.

▲ The little town of Dolores Hidalgo was the home of parish priest Miguel Hidalgo. Hidalgo rang the church bell and signalled the start of the 11 year struggle to win independence from Spanish rule.

◄ General Antonio López de Santa Anna was a vain and unscrupulous politician-soldier. His periods of incompetent rule ended in exile and disgrace after the sale of Texas and disastrous war with the United States.

▼ When the United States integrated Texas with the Union in 1845, Mexico declared war. Cerro Gordo was one of the battles fought before American forces took Mexico City and peace was declared on February 2nd, 1848.

▲ President Benito Juárez was the greatest figure of the reform period after Independence. A Zapotec Indian lawyer and dedicated Liberal patriot, he had the task of reorganising a war shattered and bankrupt country. He died of a heart attack in 1872, worn out by his incessant labours.

▼ The Hapsburg Archduke Maximilian, brother of the Austrian Emperor Franz Joseph, accepted the crown of Mexico after a French military invasion. Bitter strife led to his betrayal, capture, and execution at Querétaro on June 19th, 1867. His wife Carlota became insane and died in Europe.

▲ Porfirio Díaz controlled Mexico for 34 years. It was a long period of peace, order, and progress, for which the price was heavy. A *mestizo* from Oaxaca, Díaz was brave, intelligent, cunning, and ruthless. He stabilised the country's finances and encouraged foreign investment. But the Indians and peasants lived in misery, and liberty was abolished. Revolts in the north sparked off the Revolution which led to Díaz's fall and exile to Paris, where he died in 1915.

The Revolution

Madero's Presidency

The Mexican Revolution started on November 20th, 1910. Francisco Madero, a member of a wealthy Creole family, an idealist and humanitarian, opposed the Díaz regime and was put in prison. Díaz never understood Madero's popularity when he later released him, and rebellions began simultaneously in several parts of the country. Madero joined rebel forces in the north commanded by the former bandit Pancho Villa, whilst Emiliano Zapata led peasant raids on the rich *haciendas* in the south. Díaz fled the country on May 26th, 1911, and on November 6th Madero took over as President.

Madero, a sincere democrat, was not tough enough to control the unruly Congress. The treacherous General Victoriano Huerta then staged a coup, imprisoned Madero and his Vice-president Suárez, and made himself President. Madero was assassinated while in custody, and Huerta began a dictatorship which triggered off fierce resistance all over the country. Madero became a martyr for the cause of the rebels.

More assassinations

Civil war raged until Venustiano Carranza was able to have a new Constitution promulgated on February 5th, 1917, which is still today the basis of Mexican government.

Soon afterwards Carranza became President, but his administration failed to pass enough radical reform, and he was overthrown.

Álvaro Obregón became the next President on December 1st, 1920. A fine soldier and a shrewd politician, Obregón established measures of agrarian reform. He worked to improve Mexico's economic independence, and launched a vigorous programme to extend educational progress.

Plutarco Elías Calles succeeded Obregón as President in 1924. Their two regimes were a consolidation of the Revolution. Calles amended the Constitution to allow Obregón to succeed him for a second term of office in 1928, but Obregón was shot dead at a victory banquet in Mexico City.

The Revolutionary climax

Calles controlled succeeding presidents until the election in 1934 of General Lázaro Cárdenas. The Cárdenas regime was notable for its working class orientated policy, greatly accelerated land distribution and agrarian reforms, freedom of speech, and above all, the nationalization of the foreign-owned oil industry.

The Cárdenas presidency is generally seen to be the climax of the Revolution. This convulsion cost over a million lives and caused ruinous destruction, yet laid the foundation of a national pride and identity.

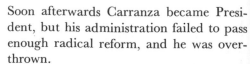

▲ This photograph of Francisco Madero, the first President of the revolution era, shows him as the unassuming and modest idealist he was. His brief period in office ended in a sordid betrayal and assassination.

▼ Pancho Villa and Emiliano Zapata, famous revolutionary heroes, met in Mexico City to discuss the struggle against Carranza's faction which they considered too conservative.

▼ Thousands of women joined the revolutionary forces and fought as bravely as their men. Adelita was a famous *soldadera*. A song about her is still sung everywhere in Mexico today.

▲ For thousands of peasants, the cry "Land and liberty!" meant leaving poverty stricken homes to fight Government troops. Many died in the merciless atrocities and massacres of their long struggle.

▶ General Plutarco Elías Calles was an able and effective President notable for his hostility to the Church. Using ruthless politics, he kept control of the country for 10 years, and ended decades of militarism.

▼ Pancho Villa was a bandit and outlaw. His hatred of oppressive governments developed his talents for leadership and revolt. Like Zapata he was assassinated and became a legend in history and song.

▲ President Lázaro Cárdenas had a very personal style of government. His humanity and love of the land made him very popular. His nationalization of the oil industry was bitterly opposed by foreign owners, but it secured Mexico's future industrial development.

37

Customs and festivals

▼ The annual September festival in honour of the Virgin of the Remedies is attended by many thousands of people. These gaily decorated towers are part of an old aqueduct which brought water to the revered Sanctuary more than 350 years ago.

Fiestas and saints

Mexican life is still based on enduring religious beliefs, and its festival days are of Indian or Catholic origin. They all have a basic theme of adoration, whether of ancient deities or of the Virgins of Guadalupe and Remedios. Every village has its fiesta to honour the patron Saint's day, and times of drought and flood are also perfectly understandable reasons for festivals in which prayers are offered for rain or sunshine.

The calendar of festival days contains nearly 100 important dates in the year, so there would be little time for work for anyone who wanted to see them all! Some fiestas go on for a week or more, when they may be called *ferias*, or fairs, and include bullfights, cockfights, and agricultural shows with rodeos.

Fireworks

All fiestas culminate in firework displays after nightfall, when everybody surrounds the *castillo*, which is the set piece of an

---

▼ The ancient town of Tepotzotlán, 40 Km. (25 miles) from Mexico City, is famous for its lovely 400 year old convent and church. Dedicated to St. Martin, it is the scene of many colourful festivals.

elaborately framed mass of fireworks towering above the eagerly waiting crowds. Equally exciting may be a *globo*, a huge balloon of innumerable tiny scraps of multicoloured paper, hung with dozens of tiny lanterns. This floats slowly into the night sky until it catches fire and explodes in a brilliant ball of flames and flashing sparks.

The year of festivals all over Mexico begins properly with the Epiphany, the Day of the Kings, when presents are traditionally given, especially where Father Christmas has not appeared! Carnival reigns over the week before Lent, and then comes Corpus Christi, memorable for the *Voladores*— Dance of the Flying Men—at Papantla, near Vera Cruz.

Independence Day on the 16th September is a time of national rejoicing as the President rings Father Hidalgo's famous Liberty Bell. All Saints' Day is an occasion for feasting in spite of its being called the Day of the Dead, when everyone goes off to the cemeteries. Finally comes Christmastide and the nine *posada* days of the search for a refuge for the infant Jesus.

The fiesta provides an excellent means of studying Mexican customs and ways of life. It allows people to realize their dreams, develop artistic instincts, and to forget the sadness of life in a contempt for death.

Some festivals and holidays

Jan 1:	New Year's Day
Jan 6:	Day of the Kings— presents are given
Holy Week:	Processions, fiestas and Passion Plays
May 1:	Labour Day
May 3:	Masons and Builders Festival
May 5:	National holiday— anniversary of Battle of Puebla
Corpus Christi:	Voladores at Papantla and processions in Mexico City
Sept 16:	Independence Day
Sept 30:	Commemoration of the birth of José María Morelos, one of the leaders in the independence movement
Oct 12:	Columbus Day
Nov 1-2:	Day of the Dead
Nov 20:	Holiday celebrating the Revolution
Dec 12:	Festival of Our Lady of Guadalupe
Dec 16-25:	Posadas and Piñatas
Dec 25:	Christmas Day

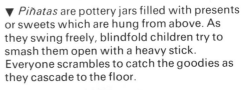

▼ *Piñatas* are pottery jars filled with presents or sweets which are hung from above. As they swing freely, blindfold children try to smash them open with a heavy stick. Everyone scrambles to catch the goodies as they cascade to the floor.

▲ Huejotzingo, near Puebla, is known for its Shrove Tuesday carnival commemorating the Mexican victory over French troops in 1862. Opposing forces take part in mock battles ending with a spectacular explosion and deafening volleys of shots.

◄ Upper class society in Mexico still includes families descended from Spanish grandees. Fashionable weddings are very formal ceremonies. Great wealth is discreetly indicated by the elegance of the women's clothes and superb jewellery.

▼ The Mexican acceptance of death is always coupled with a devout faith in the life to come. Bereaved people are conscious that the souls of the departed remain close by, and believe that the death watch ensures a safe passage for them. In spite of official opposition to the Church after the Revolution, the religious fervour of the people was not quenched.

▲ Christmas Day in Mexico is preceded by the nine nights of *posadas*, when families and friends join after dark in processions commemorating the search of Mary and Joseph for room at an inn *(posada)*. Dressed in Biblical costumes, they knock at neighbours' doors and are turned away. Only on the last night do they find a refuge, when a party of thanksgiving is enjoyed by everyone at the house which is chosen in advance.

Dynamic Mexico City

▲ Tenochtitlán is pictured as it must have appeared to the amazed Spaniards when they approached Lake Texcoco. Built amongst causeways and canals like Venice, its temples and pyramids were surrounded by markets and workshops. Archaeologists are still finding valuable remains of the Aztec capital under modern Mexico City.

▼ The heart of the city is the great Constitution Plaza, called the Zócalo. This was originally the centre of the Aztec capital Tenochtitlán. The Zócalo is now dominated by the cathedral which was begun in 1573 on the site of an earlier church built over an Aztec temple. The cathedral is a majestic building. The adjoining Sagrario Metropolitano is a separate church built in the 18th century.

Problems of growth

Mexico City's fantastic growth, to its present population of over nine million people, has created many problems for the Government. Provision of water, sewage facilities, electricity, and housing simply cannot keep up with the flow of immigrants from the rest of the country.

Squalid shanty towns blight the outskirts of a magnetic and contrasting metropolis of soaring skyscrapers, magnificent avenues, crumbling Colonial churches and palaces, and luxurious hotels and residential estates.

The Zócalo, an enormous open square, is the heart of the city. It stands over the original Aztec foundations of Tenochtitlán. The Cathedral dominates the plaza, its harmonious architectural styles reflecting the 250 years it took to build. The National Palace rose from the rubble of Moctezuma's own palace, and was first occupied in 1529 by Cortés. The famous Liberty Bell of the War of Independence hangs outside. The Bell is rung by every President on 16th September each year.

Colonial buildings

The old part of the city around the Zócalo has many Colonial churches and palaces, but most are sadly decayed and in need of restoration. The Basilica of Guadalupe is revered by Catholics as the holiest shrine of all the Americas. The site on which it was built was the scene of a miraculous vision of the Virgin in 1531.

The beautiful old Colonial villages of San Angel and Coyoacán, now within the boundary of the city, have venerable cobbled streets lined with tranquil, colourful mansions and cottages. Some were built as homes for Cortés, Alvarado, and other Spanish conquistadores.

Nearby is the contrasting ultra modern luxury estate of Pedregal, where sumptuous villas with large gardens extend over a 4,000 year old volcanic lava bed. Many prehistoric remains have been found in this area.

Elegant avenues

The Paseo de la Reforma, a magnificent tree shaded avenue, leads to Chapultepec Castle, home of the ill fated Emperor Maximilian and his tragic wife Carlota. The beautiful park contains the Museum of Anthropology, acknowledged as the finest in the world. The twelve mile long Avenida Insurgentes arrows through elegant suburbs and shopping centres.

▲ Like many cities the Mexican capital has its slums, with crowded tenements and desperately poor people. Many of those who live here have sought to escape the poverty of country villages, but their numbers are so great that jobs are difficult to find. These children appear happy enough, but their future may be hard and discouraging. The Government sees the danger of excessive population concentration and is encouraging new industrial zones where work and homes are being created.

Places to visit in Mexico City

1 National Museum of Anthropology

2 Cathedral

3 Palace of Fine Arts

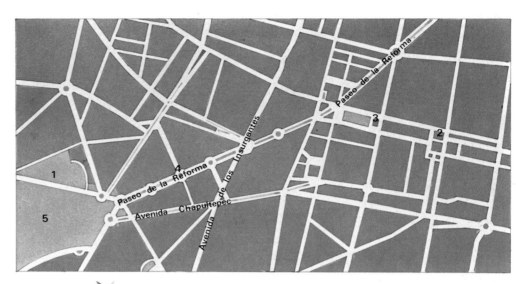

4 Column of Independence

5 Chapultepec Park and Castle

▲ The Latin American Tower is the tallest building in Mexico. Thanks to its floating foundation chambers, it is immune from earthquakes.

◄ Chapultepec Park is a beautiful expanse of woods, meadows, gardens and lakes. There is an imposing castle on the hill.

41

Agriculture and rural life

▼ Mexico is one of the three major Arabica type coffee producers in the world. These coffee beans drying on a patio floor are grown in the tropical south and may well be destined for the growing export market.

▼ The potential for livestock production growth has only recently been properly understood. Traditional cattle grazing areas in the dry northern pastures have very poor capacity, and American type feed lots like this now flourish in the rich grasslands of the plains of Vera Cruz.

The end of feudalism

The structure of agriculture and its very low production were major reasons for the Revolution of 1910. Some 97% of the land was in the hands of a few thousand owners. About 2% belonged to half a million small-holders, and the remainder was communal property held by townships. An antiquated feudal system was supported by a government controlled by the powerful landed families. Agriculture was little diversified and production was variable.

The 1917 Constitution established that the nation is the original owner of the land and can impose such conditions as the public interest may require. Agrarian laws have been responsible for the distribution of about 85 million hectares (1 hectare equals $2\frac{1}{2}$ acres) of land amongst nearly three

million farmers. However, there are still too many landless countrymen, and because farmland is increasingly scarce, this poses a serious problem. A large part of the rural community may well have to be moved to areas of expanding industry and commerce.

Increasing production

Thanks to vast irrigation projects financed by the Government, Mexico's arable land has been increased to about 30 million hectares. Agricultural production steadily increases, and is becoming more diversified. There is a wide variety of crops, the most important of which are maize, wheat, beans, cotton, sugar cane, coffee, rice, and sorghum. Export commodities are being encouraged and now include strawberries, melons, tomatoes, avocados, and grapefruit.

Animal husbandry has developed greatly in recent years, and beef cattle raising is now extending beyond the traditional northern dry pastures.

Forestry is under strict State control, as is planning for conservation and expansion for construction lumber and cellulose. Other valuable products are fibres, wax, oils such as turpentine, and chicle, the raw material for making chewing gum.

◄ Maize has been the staple crop of Mexico for thousands of years, and is often still harvested by hand on peasant-owned plots where mechanization would not be feasible.

▼ Whilst many *peones* work on communal lands called *ejidos*, some manage to keep their own smallholdings, aided by local farm banks with low interest loans.

▲ A typical pastoral scene dominated by the snowy crest of Popocatépetl. Many Mexican sheep show their cross-bred descent from Spanish Manchego and Merino breeds.

▶ Beautiful Lake Pátzcuaro in Michoacán is famous for its delicate white fish and the unique butterfly nets of its fishermen. These Tarasc Indians control their nets with a pole between the "wings" so that they glide silently under the fish.

▼ The rapid growth of Mexico's population has made increased food production vital. Mechanization, irrigation and fertilizers are transforming backward rural areas into prosperous farmlands with a wide range of crops for home and export.

Crafts and industry

Handicraft skills

Mexico has always been a country in which handicraft skills have important values in general social life. The Government finances the conservation, protection, and encouragement of this vital aspect of the national culture. Some two million families, mostly in rural areas and small towns, are involved in the production of a wide range of objects in daily use or of high artistic quality.

The leading centres of handicrafts are of original Indian foundation, with later Spanish influence. These now have training schools and workshops, exhibitions, warehouses, and, of course, markets. Export campaigns maintain overseas sales to many countries, especially the U.S.A.

Pottery work has the largest number of craftsmen and includes the famous Talavera ware, terra cotta objects, and the beautiful black clay ware of Oaxaca.

Textiles and silver

Handloomed and woven textiles, mostly of cotton, often retain their ancient Indian designs and colours, whether for everyday use or for high fashion garments. Hard fibres such as palm leaves and sisal are used to make bags, belts, hats, and carpets.

As the world's leading silver producer, Mexico has a great silverwork tradition. Table services, cutlery, ornamental pieces, rings and jewellery are still made following the ancient Indian processes. Goldwork also reaches the highest standards of skilled art.

Modern industrial activity

In recent years industry has become the most dynamic sector of the Mexican economy, and has shown a yearly growth rate of over eight per cent. It is aided by Federal promotional measures, direct investment, fiscal incentives, and protection policies designed to stimulate production and reduce imports.

The principal extractive industry is oil, a decisive factor in economic development. The oil industry employs over 70,000 people and provides 90 per cent of the nation's energy. Petróleos Mexicanos is the sole organization responsible for every aspect of this vital industry and its processed by-products.

Mining is an old established industry. Mexico has very abundant supplies of valuable raw materials, including silver, iron ore, sulphur, zinc, manganese, lead, fluorite, copper, coal, and some gold.

Electrical power production maintains great growth rates, supporting the chemical industry's vigorous expansion in the manufacture of sulphuric acid, synthetic fibres, insecticides, and fertilisers. Motor cars are now made through licensing agreements with Ford, Chrysler, Volkswagen, Renault, and others.

▲ Tourism is an essential source of foreign exchange for Mexico, and is dominated by the Americans. Acapulco and its splendid beaches attract visitors from all over the world.

▼ The crafts of Mexican Indians are endowed with artistic value where they have not been corrupted by tourists' tastes. Hip weaving fortunately continues as an important cottage industry in many villages.

◄ Since the nationalization of oil in 1938, Pemex (Petróleos Mexicanos) has controlled all aspects of this giant industry. This refinery has a vital function in the supply of energy to keep Mexico working.

▼ Hand-blown glassware, especially from Jalisco, is a popular buy. Cut glass often has the traditional pumpkin seed "pip" decoration. Stained glass windows are radiant with vivid Indian colours.

▲ Several varieties of agave plants thrive in Mexico. These include henequen, the fibres of which are called sisal hemp. Yucatan is the leading producer of this raw material for ropes, mats, and hammocks.

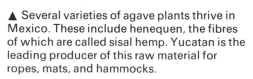

▼ The art of gold and silversmiths reached a high level long before the arrival of the Spaniards. Some centres such as Taxco have streets of metal and jewel workers' shops with amazingly low prices for exquisitely designed pieces.

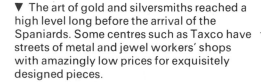

▲ Pottery is one of the oldest crafts and in Mexico the potters have innumerable examples of their ancestors' work to emulate. The range is enormous, from objects in common use, to beautifully painted decorative work. Apart from Talavera ware from Puebla, most of the best pottery still comes from old Indian villages.

Music and dance

▶ These Aztec dancers at Guadalupe Basilica are wearing authentic copies of brilliantly coloured costumes worn centuries ago. Their dancing style has always been formal and controlled, producing some of the loveliest of all Indian dances.

▼ The Ballet Folklorico has done much to preserve traditional Indian dances. They use authentic costumes and music created through meticulous historical and archae-ological research. Some dances are adapted to ballet, with choreography based on stories of the ancient gods and emperors.

▲ The Dance of the Quetzal is seen at its bes in the south, where the beautiful, streamer-tailed quetzal bird lives in the jungles. This magnificent head-dress represents its multi-coloured feathers, and in ancient times entire costumes were made of coloured featherwor by the Indians.

Primitive ceremonies

Fiestas always played a vital part in the life of the ancient Indian world, and they were celebrated, as today, with music, singing and dancing. Sacrifices to the gods, successful battles and hunts, weddings and deaths, were all occasions for ritual ceremonies in which everybody played a part.

Every region still has its own distinctive musical rhythm—*Huapangos* and *Sones* in Vera Cruz; *Jaranas* in Yucatan; *Canacuas* in Michoacán; *Sandungas* in Tehuantepéc; and many others. The *Jarabe Tapatío* of Jalisco has long been recognized as the national folkloric dance.

Corridos are very typically Mexican—long recitations in witty verse sung with simple melodies indefinitely repeated. They were strongly stimulated by the Revolution. Strolling bands of musicians called *mariachis* play these and other popular songs, especially in Mexico City and Guadalajara.

Folk dancers

The fantastic costumes and masks worn by folk dancers are survivals from very remote times. Typical are the *Viejitos* (Old Men) of Michoacán; *Los Moros* (Moors) wearing turbans and black masks, and the extravagant Oaxacan head decorations of tropical birds' feathers. The famous Ballet Folklorico stages authentic shows of traditional songs and dances with immaculate choreography and dazzling costumes.

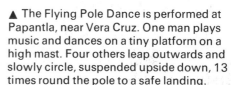

▲ The Flying Pole Dance is performed at Papantla, near Vera Cruz. One man plays music and dances on a tiny platform on a high mast. Four others leap outwards and slowly circle, suspended upside down, 13 times round the pole to a safe landing.

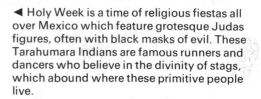

◄ Holy Week is a time of religious fiestas all over Mexico which feature grotesque Judas figures, often with black masks of evil. These Tarahumara Indians are famous runners and dancers who believe in the divinity of stags, which abound where these primitive people live.

An artistic tradition

Indian artistic genius

The Spaniards encouraged Indian painting and sculpture after the Conquest, as the friars soon realized that the natives already had a highly developed natural bent for visual expression. Their frescoes, oil paintings, wood carvings, and masonry decorated the churches and monasteries that were built all over the country as the Spaniards extended their domain. The art of fresco mural painting had been used in many pre-Columbian buildings, notably at the Maya temple of Bonampak. This tradition was spectacularly revived after the Revolution, and continues its impact today.

During the Colonial period, most painting became stifled by European trends, and the awakening of a truly national artistic conscience began with Doctor Atl (1887-1964), the founder of the Mexican school. He was the bridge between the objective painting of the past and the subjective vision of reality which marks modern art. Dr Atl was a modern pioneer of murals and a great innovator of new ideas and techniques.

Revolutionary art

In 1921 José Vasconcelos took over a newly created Ministry of Public Education and Fine Arts. His vigour and encouragement led to the era of the great muralists Diego Rivera, José Clemente Orozco, and David Alfaro Siqueiros. Their artistic development sprang directly from the political transformation of their country, and achieved a unique degree of success and influence. Their monumental work was almost all officially commissioned, and they became visual educators, inspiring a still mainly illiterate people with revolutionary ideals.

The last masterpiece of this trio is the gigantic Polyforum Cultural of David Siqueiros in Mexico City. It is a stunning creation of sculpture combined with painting of three dimensional composition, viewed from a vast turntable. *The March of Humanity* murals cover a vast area of acrylic and metal panels, and one can but marvel at this immense work of genius.

▲ Diego Rivera explored the riches of his country's history throughout his painting life, and became one of its truly inspired interpreters. His murals in the National Palace are universally acclaimed for their flowing draughtsmanship and colour. This picture is a vision of his Indian world.

▼ This fine example of Siqueiros' work on the National University headquarters is a powerful propaganda symbol of teachers guiding a student to a future in which "his training will give fruit to the people who provide the seed". Siqueiros was a master of many technical innovations.

◄ The chaotic and tragic themes of much of Orozco's work are superbly shown by his murals in the Hospital of Jesus, founded by Cortés in 1574. The artist is seen working on *The Four Horsemen of the Apocalypse,* a picture typical of his deep contempt for man's greed and cruelty.

▼ Felix Candela is an engineering genius and architect, famous for his extremely thin but strong parabolic shells of concrete. A brilliant sun creates striking contrasts of light and shadow at this fashionable Mexico City restaurant, thus providing a splendid talking point over its tables.

▲ The Museum of Modern Art in Chapultepec Park contains the work of both Mexican and foreign artists. This sculpture resembles a primitive Indian deity such as may be seen on many pre-Columbian archaeological sites.

► The beautiful baroque church of Santa María Tonanzintla, near Puebla, is a wholly Indian concept of Christian glory. Dark skinned angels and cherubs are carved in a mass of flowers and fruit streaming everywhere in a dazzling blaze of colour.

The Mexican influence

Foreign exploitation

The Revolution profoundly changed the attitudes of the Great Powers, which had hitherto looked upon Mexico as a kind of vassal state. The country's valuable natural resources such as silver, gold, and oil were all exploited with enormous profits for British and American companies. In this sense the Revolution is still in progress, and the Government insists that all development of its vital resources should remain under Mexican control.

Mexico now stands out as a Latin American country which has had great success in dealing with racial integration and in avoiding conflicts of white and Indian cultures. Her Government is a staunch supporter of the United Nations but opposes interference in the domestic affairs of other countries. She is one of the very few Latin American countries with relatively modest armed forces.

Trade and finance

Mexico is a leading advocate of free trade associations, constantly works to increase aid for the developing nations, and has won respect for her policies of political moderation and non-alignment. Even the United States has modified her attitude towards Mexico.

The Mexican peso is one of the world's most stable currencies, and is so highly regarded in international banking that it is used by the International Monetary Fund for financial support to other countries, including the United Kingdom.

Archaeology and architecture

In the fields of archaeology, architecture, medicine, and painting, Mexico is acknowledged as a world leader. In no other country is archaeology so much a part of national culture. The Museum of Anthropology has no equal, and houses unique and fascinating displays of ancient civilizations. Mexican architects such as Marío Pani and Félix Candela display a virtuosity and technical skill admired by all who deplore the uniformity of European and American cities today. The Plaza of the Three Cultures triumphantly shows the continuity of the Mexican genius for building.

▲ Mexico strongly opposes interference in other countries' national affairs. Years of exploitation of her own resources by foreign powers left their mark. These students are demonstrating against the U.S.A.

▶ The internationally famous film director Luis Buñuel, although Spanish born, conveys the atmosphere of his adopted country, Mexico, in his brilliant films.

▼ Mexico's fine climate and facilities for sports attracted the Olympic Games in 1968 and the World Soccer Championship in 1970. The Olympic sailing contests were held at Acapulco, where international fishing and sailing competitions are regular events.

► Until the discovery and colonization of Mexico, Europeans had never seen maize, beans, chocolate, turkeys, tomatoes, avocados, chilli peppers, and peanuts. Many other fruits and vegetables native to Mexico are still not known abroad. Mexican flowers common in gardens of the world are dahlias, zinnias, marigolds, poinsettias, and lobelias.

◄ The National Museum of Anthropology and History is a monument to a proud past, and houses magnificent displays of the ancient civilizations. The London *Times* described it as 50 years ahead of any other museum in the world. Archaeologists and historians of many nationalities work in Mexico, learning new skills and techniques in interpretation of the past.

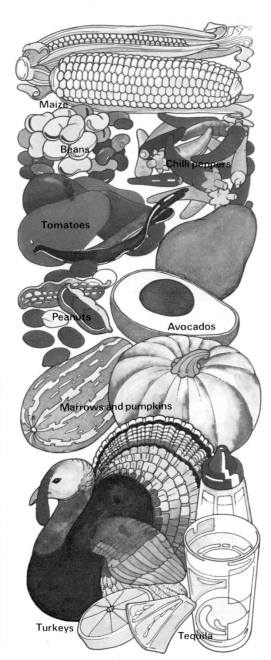

Maize

Beans

Chilli peppers

Tomatoes

Peanuts

Avocados

Marrows and pumpkins

Turkeys

Tequila

▲ The vigorous and also the declining cultures of the various Mexican Indian groups provide valuable material for genetic studies. These scientists are supervising taste tests of liquids and foods for research on how integration into modern society affects the Indians. The Lacandones of the picture are almost extinct descendants of the Maya. Only about 200 pure blooded members of the tribe still survive in the depths of the jungles and swampy rivers of Chiapas.

► A feature of Mexican agronomy has been an improvement of vital crop seeds such as wheat, which are being used in some Asian and European countries. The FAO has stated that Mexican dwarf wheats are of outstanding importance to world food growing. Dr Jacobo Ortega, a well known agronomist, is seen here teaching students from Iran, Afghanistan, Philippines, and Pakistan about new kinds of grain suitable for their countries.

A changing society

▶ "Make sure that the seed of culture germinates in Mexican soil" is the message of this remarkable poster. The alphabet letters symbolise the vital importance of literacy in an advancing nation.

◀ These Mixtec Indians are waiting outside a clinic for medical treatment. Practical help like this is provided by an Indigenous Institute which is also responsible for educational and training facilities to enable the Indians to improve their living standards.

▼ Luis Echeverría, who was president from 1970 to 1976, was a vigorous and outspoken third world leader. His constant travels not only promoted Mexican trade but have led to greater Latin American unity.

Population growth

The immensity of the changes in Mexico which have occurred this century can be understood from a few simple facts and figures. Seventy years ago Mexican society was headed by rich landowners who were the masters of desperately poor people working on huge haciendas and in the mines. The total population, although growing, was less than fourteen million.

Today, with about 61 million people, the country has a middle class representing a substantial part of its society. More than three-fifths of the population now lives in the cities, over nine million in the vast metropolis of the capital alone.

Such a rapid increase in population in what was a poor and war shattered country created many problems. Some rural areas still have not received the benefits of modern farming systems, and many villages have uneconomic *ejidos*—communal plots of land worked as for centuries past. Many Indian communities find it difficult to assimilate new techniques. Young people leave their villages to seek work in the cities, often ending up in shanty slums.

◀ Electric power is so essential to Mexico's economic development that every effort is being made to extend the gridlines. Some sparsely populated desert lands still lack the mains power seen being erected over an agave plantation.

▼ Middle and upper class Mexicans enjoy idling in pavement cafés just as much as Europeans. But this life style only recently began to flourish with the advent of prosperous city suburbs. The climate makes this a pleasant way to relax and exchange the latest gossip.

The persistent campaigns to improve agricultural output, and extensive land reclamation projects, have transformed deserts and jungles into thriving farms and ranches. The Indigenous Institute gives aid to backward communities, providing them with schools, teachers, doctors, agricultural experts, and other services.

Cities which have grown too fast have to cope with the assimilation of thousands of illiterate immigrants from the villages, who live in shanty towns rife with disease and crime. Great efforts are being made to combat this social blight, but it will be a long and expensive struggle to achieve any significant improvement. Nevertheless, even from such discouraging environments youngsters emerge who become doctors, teachers, engineers, and businessmen.

A hopeful future

Industrial development is now expanding very quickly, especially in chemicals and petro-chemicals, steel, fertilizers, sulphur, and agricultural machinery. This has helped to create more jobs at all levels. Exports and investments from abroad are now playing a vital part in the economic growth.

The outlook for a steadily increasing number of Mexicans is one of hope and some prosperity. But for many others the road will continue to be a long and hard one. The people of Mexico are the true heirs of the Revolution, and their determination should make Madero's dream a reality.

▲ In spite of the many benefits of Mexico's progress, the sheer size and the geographical obstacles of the country have created uneven stages of development. It has the world's largest water barrages and vast irrigation zones, but there are still areas without piped water, and scenes like this are not uncommon. Daily washing of clothes and bodies is an Indian tradition unchanged by the arrival of habitually dirty Europeans.

▼ Tremendous efforts are being made to clear the rotting slum areas of the capital. Colourful new housing blocks surrounded by gardens give both parents and children renewed vigour and hope for their future.

Reference
Human and physical geography

Annual rainfall of Mexico

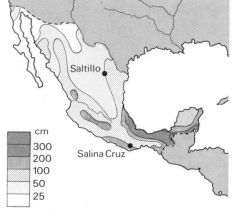

cm
- 300
- 200
- 100
- 50
- 25

Mexico has three basic climatic zones:
1. **Rainy tropical** with mean temperatures over 18°C and annual rainfall over 75 cms.
2. **Rainy sub-tropical** which includes middle and upper slopes of mountain ranges and plateaux. Mean temperatures are over 18°C in warmer months and over 0°C in winter. Annual rainfall is between 60 and 100 cms, with yearly variations.
3. **Arid** with rainfall ranging between 20 cms and 60 cms per year, but falling to less than 10 cms in desert areas. Altitude creates a great range of temperatures, and 40°C is exceeded in some parts.

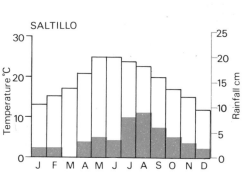

SALTILLO

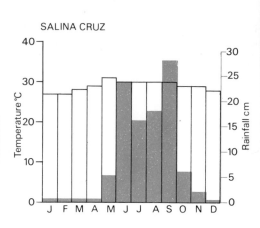

SALINA CRUZ

FACTS AND FIGURES
The land and people

Full title: The United Mexican States.

Position: Between 32°43'N and 14°33'N, and 117°08'W and 86°46'W. Mexico is part of the North American continent, bordered by the United States of America to the north, and by Guatemala and Belize to the southeast.

Area: 1,967,183 sq. km. (758,259 sq. miles), exclusive of islands.

Population: 56,500,000 (1974)

Capital: Mexico D.F. (Population 9 million).

Language: Spanish, but numerous Indian groups still speak their own languages.

Religion: Roman Catholic, but there is freedom of worship.

Political system: Representative federal republic. Executive power is exercised by the President, who is elected for 6 years. Legislative power is exercised by the Congress of the Union, consisting of a Chamber of Deputies and a Senate. Judicial authority is invested in the Supreme Court of Justice and Federal courts.

International organizations: Mexico is a member of the United Nations and the Latin American Free Trade Association (LAFTA).

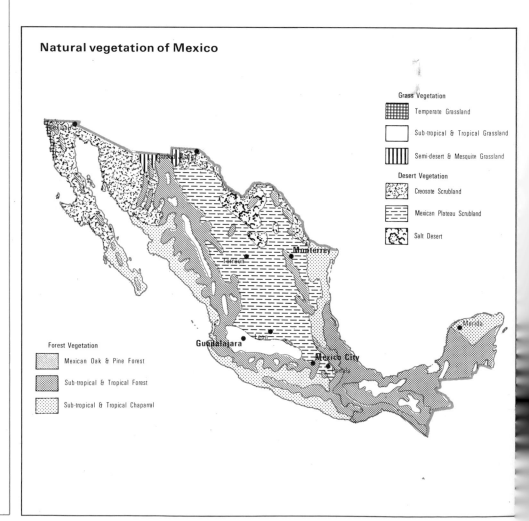

Natural vegetation of Mexico

Grass Vegetation
- Temperate Grassland
- Sub-tropical & Tropical Grassland
- Semi-desert & Mesquite Grassland

Desert Vegetation
- Creosote Scrubland
- Mexican Plateau Scrubland
- Salt Desert

Forest Vegetation
- Mexican Oak & Pine Forest
- Sub-tropical & Tropical Forest
- Sub-tropical & Tropical Chaparral

The population density

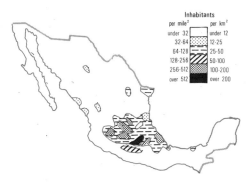

In 1976 the population of Mexico was estimated at 61,100,000. Census figures show that the population is growing at an annual rate of about 3.4%, giving a doubling of population in 20 years. The 1970 census reported 48,313,000 inhabitants, so there should be about 100,000,000 Mexicans in 1990. The population density is greatest in the central States. Eight central States with a combined area of only 6·6% of Mexico's territory had 37·7% of the total population in 1970. By contrast, six northern States covering 43·1% of the country were inhabited by only 12·1% of the total population. Nearly 50% of the total population of Mexico is under the age of 14.

Population of principal towns

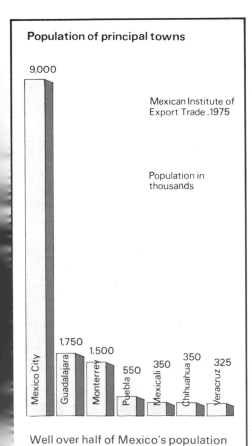

Well over half of Mexico's population now lives in the cities. Nearly one-sixth of the population lives in Mexico City.

The Mexican system of government

PRESIDENT of the REPUBLIC

ADMINISTRATION — LEGISLATION — JUDICIARY

MINISTERS of STATE — AUTONOMOUS AGENCIES

FEDERATION of STATES

TERRITORIES

FEDERAL DISTRICT

CONGRESS of the UNION

SENATE (Elected by direct vote for 6 years)

CHAMBER of DEPUTIES (Elected by direct vote for 3 years)

SUPREME COURT of JUSTICE

FEDERAL COURTS

Political organization

Officially, Mexico is called the United Mexican States. It is a representative federal republic consisting of 31 States, and a Federal District.

The Constitution, ratified in Querétaro on February 5th, 1917, is the law of the land. It establishes freedom of worship, although the great majority of Mexicans are Roman Catholic. Church and State have been separate since 1857.

The government functions under three branches: the executive, legislative, and judicial divisions, whose powers are defined in the Constitution.

Executive power

Executive power is exercised by the President, who is chief of state and of the government. He is elected by universal suffrage and secret ballot for a term of 6 years and may not be re-elected. The age for voting is now 18 years.

The President performs his duties through 16 Ministries, 2 Departments, an Attorney General, and a number of autonomous agencies. The autonomous agencies operate with their own funds and are endowed with special functions.

Legislative authority

Legislative authority is performed by the Congress of the Union, constituted by the Senate and the Chamber of Deputies. Deputies are elected by direct vote for a 3 year period and represent about every 200,000 inhabitants. Senators are also elected by direct vote for a 6 year period, each State sending 2 representatives to the Senate.

Judicial authority

The judicial authority is entrusted with the administration of justice at federal level. The top ranking body is the Supreme Court of Justice, composed of life members appointed by the President.

The Mexican government is a federation of States which are sovereign in their internal affairs. They have their own administrations elected by direct vote, and follow the federal pattern in division of powers. The Federal District is governed by a Regent appointed by the President. The Federal District is where the main government offices are located (Mexico City in fact). It should be noted that it is always properly referred to, and addressed as Mexico D.F. The *State* of Mexico is quite separate and has as its capital the town of Toluca.

Reference
History

MAIN EVENTS IN MEXICAN HISTORY

B.C.

25000-10000	Nomad hunters arrive from northern part of American Continent.
7000-2000	First agricultural settlements.
1800-1300	Village farms established with improved varieties of primitive corn, pumpkins, beans, and chilli peppers.
1300-800	Archaic settlements with pottery and stone objects at Copilco (Mexico City) and Tlapacoya.
800-200	More archaic centres with beginning of monumental religious architecture at Cuicuilco, Teotihuacán Phase I, and Monte Albán (Zapotecs).
200	Early Maya architecture begins. Teotihuacán Phase II, with building of Temple of Quetzalcóatl.

A.D.

162	Earliest dated object—statuette of possible Olmec origin found in Tuxtla.
300	Beginnings of Maya dated steles (carved stone pillars).
400	Teotihuacán Phase III, including great Palace of Quetzalpapalotl, begun. Monte Albán's unique decorative friezes sculpted.
600	Uxmal (Yucatan) ceremonial centre begun.
700	Early Nahua tribes settle in Central Mexico.
800	Temple of the Warriors begun at Chichén Itzá (Yucatan).
856	Foundation of huge ceremonial centre of Tula by Toltecs.
889	Last dated Maya record at Uaxactún.
900	Foundation of Culhuacán in Valley of Mexico by Toltecs.
1000	Toltecs reach Maya city of Chichén Itzá and combine their architectural genius with that of the Maya.
1158	Fall of Tula to Chichimecan invaders from the north.
1200	Zapotecs begin construction of religious centre of Mitla, in Oaxaca province.
1220	Foundation of Cholula (near Puebla), believed to have the largest pyramid in the world.
1300	Nahua tribes settle at an island in Lake Texcoco in the Valley of Mexico.
1325	Aztecs settle in Lake Texcoco under their chief Tenoch, thus founding Tenochtitlán on the site of modern Mexico City.
900-1521	Maya "New Empire".
1517	Francisco Hernandez de Córdoba lands at Yucatan.
1518	Juan de Grijalva explores Gulf of Mexico coasts.
1519	Hernán Cortés lands at Ulúa, near Vera Cruz, and reaches Aztec capital, Tenochtitlán, after heavy fighting and captures Emperor Moctezuma.
1520	Cortés defeated by Aztecs and forced to retreat. Moctezuma killed by his own people.
1521	Recapture of Tenochtitlán by Cortés after long siege. New Aztec Emperor Cuauhtémoc taken prisoner. Tenochtitlán destroyed and new city of Mexico begun on the ruins of the old.
1524	Cuauhtémoc executed by Cortés.
1525	Cortés named Captain-General and Governor of New Spain.
1528	Cortés returns to Spain for two years.
1535	Arrival of the first Viceroy, Don Antonio de Mendoza.
1564	Juan de Legazpi sails from Acapulco to the Philippines and founds Manila. Beginning of regular trading route between Mexico and the Far East.
1568	Drake and Hawkins raid Vera Cruz harbour.
1778	San Francisco, California, founded as northern limit of the Spanish colonial rule.
1810	Miguel Hidalgo rings the bell of his church, signalling the start of the War of Independence.
1811	Hidalgo executed at Chihuahua.
1813	José María Morelos makes first attempt to draft a Constitution for an independent Mexico.
1815	Execution of Morelos. General Vicente Guerrero takes command of rebel forces.
1821	Agustín de Iturbide joins Guerrero to sign Plan of Iguala, and the last Viceroy concedes Mexico's independence.
1822	Iturbide has himself proclaimed Agustín I, Emperor of Mexico.
1823	Iturbide forced to abdicate and exiled.
1824	Federal Constitution of the Mexican Republic promulgated. Guadalupe Victoria becomes the first President.
1828	Vicente Guerrero assumes Presidency after a revolt.
1829	Spanish forces attempt to recover Mexico, but capitulate to General Santa Anna.
1830	General Anastasio Bustamante usurps Presidency.
1832	Santa Anna elected President but declines office and Gomez Farías takes office.
1836	Santa Anna defeats Texan forces at the Alamo, but is soon afterwards crushed by the Texans. The secession of Texas from Mexico follows.
1837	The "Pastry War" against French forces at Vera Cruz ends in victory for Santa Anna.
1846	America declares war on Mexico and American troops invade.
1848	Treaty of Guadalupe Hidalgo. Mexico forced to give up half of its territory for 15 million dollars.
1853	Santa Anna again President for the last time before exile.
1857	A new federalist constitution is approved under President Ignacio Comonfort.
1858	War of the Reform begins. General Felix Zuloaga seizes power in Mexico City for the Conservatives. The Liberals elect Benito Juárez as legitimate President at Vera Cruz
1861	President Juárez takes over a bankrupt country and announces suspension of foreign debts.
1862	Allied forces of Britain, Spain, and France land at Vera Cruz. French defeated at Battle of Puebla.
1863	Large French army under General Forey takes Mexico City and establishes Mexican Empire. Throne offered to Archduke Maximilian, brother of Austrian Emperor Francis Joseph.
1864	Maximilian and his wife Carlota enthroned as Emperor and Empress of Mexico.
1866	French Emperor Napoleon III decides to withdraw French forces from Mexico.
1867	French troops leave Mexico. Juarist forces defeat Maximilian at Querétaro, where the Emperor and his generals Miramón and Mejía are executed. Juárez resumes as President.
1872	Juárez dies of a heart attack. Succeeded as President by Lerdo de Tejada.
1876	General Porfirio Díaz becomes President.
1910	Revolution breaks out simultaneously in Puebla and Chihuahua.
1911	Díaz resigns and goes into exile. Francisco Madero becomes President.
1913	Madero murdered. General Victoriano Huerta illegally takes over the Presidency and establishes a reign of terror.
1917	New political constitution promulgated at Querétaro. Venustiano Carranza becomes President.
1920	Collapse of Carranza regime. General Álvaro Obregón takes office.
1924	Plutarco Elías Calles elected President.
1928	Obregón assassinated, and puppet Presidents take office for two year terms under the control of Calles.

1934	Lázaro Cárdenas elected President.
1938	Nationalization of the oil industry.
1940	Manuel Ávila Camacho elected President.
1946	Miguel Alemán Valdés elected President.
1952	Adolfo Ruiz Cortines elected President.
1958	Adolfo López Mateos elected President.
1964	Gustavo Díaz Ordaz elected President.
1968	The Olympic Games are held in Mexico.
1970	Luis Echeverría Alvarez elected President.
1975	Queen Elizabeth II visits Mexico.
1976	Jose Lopez Portilla elected President.

The Arts

PAINTING
Baltasar de Echave el Viejo (1548-1630): Known as the "Mexican Titian". Excelled in large paintings for churches.
Cristobal de Villalpando (1649-1714): Popular artist notable for immense paintings decorating Mexico City Cathedral.
Miguel Cabrera (1695-1768): An Oaxacan Indian muralist and engraver on copper, of highly individual style.
Francisco Eduardo Tresguerras (1765-1833) · Architect, sculptor, engraver, and painter who designed and decorated strikingly beautiful churches.
José María Velasco (1840-1912): Landscape painter notable for very fine pictures of Valley of Mexico.
José Guadalupe Posada (1852-1913): Superb engraver and cartoonist famous for his "death's head" themes.
Gerardo Murillo—known as Dr. Atl (1875-1964): Outstanding muralist and landscape painter. His volcano pictures show brilliant mastery of colour.
José Clemente Orozco (1883-1940).
Diego Rivera (1886-1957).
David Alfaro Siqueiros (1898-1974): The three great muralists of the Revolutionary period.
Rufino Tamayo (b. 1899): Muralist and easel painter whose unique semi-abstract style and vivid colours have made him world famous.
Juan O'Gorman (b. 1905): Architect and muralist whose masterpiece is the Library of the National University of Mexico.

ARCHITECTURE
Manuel Tolsá (1755-1816): Famous for severely classical style buildings such as School of Mines, Mexico City. Sculptor of huge equestrian statue of Spanish King Charles IV, and *Faith, Hope and Charity* group on Mexico City Cathedral.
Mario Pani Brilliant modern designer and planner of many outstanding buildings. His unique Plaza of the Three Cultures is an imaginative exercise in artistic and practical town planning.
Félix Candela Civil engineering genius and designer whose daring use of curved concrete shells is shown to perfection in Church of Our Lady of Miracles, Mexico City.

LITERATURE
Juana Inés de la Cruz (1651-1695): Latin America's foremost woman poet. Her sonnets, lyrics, and elegies reveal acute intelligence and a deeply passionate nature curbed by her life in a convent.
Enrique González Martínez (1871-1951): Great poet of Modernist movement with an austere and serene style rarely seen in Mexican writing.
Mariano Azuela (1873-1952): Novelist who based his works on episodes of the Revolution. *Those Below* translated into many languages.
José Vasconcelos (1882-1950): Philosopher, statesman, and writer deeply influenced by the struggles of the Revolution.
Antonio Caso (1883-1946): Philosopher and poet who championed freedom of thought and expression.
Alfonso Reyes (1889-1959): Mexico's greatest literary figure of the century. Philosopher, poet, critic, essayist, and translator. *Vision of Anáhuac* is a masterpiece in verse.
Francisco Rojas González (1905-1951): Novelist and short story writer whose *El Diosero* is universally admired.
Jaime Torres Bodet (b. 1902): Politician, poet, essayist, and critic. *Three Inventors of Reality, Time and Memory in Proust's Work, Ruben Dario—Abyss and Summit,* Memoirs *—Years Against Time.*
Xavier Villaurutia (1903-1950): Poet, dramatist, and theatre director. *Death's Nostalgia* and *Song of Spring* are best known verse collections. Plays include: *The Incandescent Error, Poor Blue Chin, Invitation to Death.*
Salvador Novo (b. 1904): Poet, essayist, and dramatist, a master of satire and irony. *The Elegant Woman, Eight Columns, The War of the Fat Ones.* Founded influential Ulysses Theatre with Xavier Villaurutia in 1928.
Rodolfo Usigli (b. 1905): Mexico's leading dramatist. *The Gesticulator, Crown of Shadows, The Boy and the Mist, Crown of Light.*
Fernando Benítez (b. 1910): Essayist and novelist. *The Old King, Poisoned Water.* Wrote highly important study *The Indians of Mexico.*
José Revueltas (b. 1914): Novelist with deeply tragic sense of life. *Walls of Water, The Human Struggle, The Mistake.*
Octavio Paz (b. 1914): Poet, essayist, and philosopher of world reputation. His *Labyrinth of Solitude* is a remarkable study of the Mexican mind and character.
Carlos Fuentes (b. 1928): Novelist and short story writer. Many of his books are international best sellers: *The Most Transparent Region, The Death of Artemio Cruz, The Sacred Zone, The Birthdays.* Plays: *All Cats are Grey, The One-eyed Man is King.*

MUSIC
Manuel Ponce (1886-1948): Prolific composer of piano, chamber, and symphonic music. Director of National University School of Music.
Silvestre Revueltas (1899-1940): Violinist, conductor, and composer. Ballet music for *La Coronela,* suite *Sensemaya,* and scores for many films are richly expressive and passionate.
Carlos Chavez (b. 1899): Director of Academy of Music and Mexico Symphony Orchestra. Created picturesque symphonies, ballets, and choral works. His *Indian Symphony* and *Antigone,* and opera *Panfilo and Laureta* are world renowned.
Miguel Bernal Jimenez (1910-1957): Composer and teacher. Wrote *Tata Vasco* opera. Founded Morelia Children's Choir which is seen and heard all over the world.
Concha Michel (b. 1907): Eminent musicographer and founder of Morelia Folklore Institute. Has devoted her life to studies of Indian popular music.

Guide to pronunciation

Mexican Spanish closely resembles that of Spain. The main differences are the absence of the Castilian lisp for *z* and *c* sounds, and the quite high percentage of Indian words.

Key to vowel sounds:
Spanish vowel	English sound
a	ah
e	ay
i	ee
o	oh
u	oo
y	ee

Examples:
Acapulco—Ah-kah-POOL-koh
Aztec—AHS-tehk
Hernán Cortés—Ehr-NAHN Kor-TESS
Guadalajara—Hwah-dah-lah-HAR-rah
Hacienda—Ahs-ee-EHN-dah
Benito Juárez—Beh-NEE-toh HWAH-ress
México (Méjico)—MEH-hee-koh
Moctezuma—Mohk-teh-SOO-mah
Oaxaca—Wah-HAH-kah
Tequila—Teh-KEE-lah

Reference
The Economy

FACTS AND FIGURES

Gross Domestic Product: 1,221 billion pesos (1976).
Economic Growth Rate: about 4% per year (1978, estimated).
Main source of income:
Agriculture: maize, wheat, coffee, sugar cane, beans, bananas, alfalfa, rice, tomatoes, cattle, flowers, cotton.
Fishing: shrimp, oyster, sardine, tuna, red snapper, grouper, sawfish.
Mining: silver, gold, zinc, lead, copper, iron, manganese, antimony, sulphur, coal, barite, graphite.
Oil: petrol, kerosene, diesel oil, fuel oil, asphalt, lubricants, paraffin, petrochemicals.
Industry: iron and steel, chemicals, synthetic fibres, insecticides, cement, motor vehicles, textiles, electrical equipment, fertilisers.
Main trading partners: United States (about 60%), Japan and Common Market countries.
Currency: The peso. Exchange rate fixed against U.S. dollar at $1 = 22.7 pesos (February 1979). £1 = 45 pesos (approx).

The Economy

Mexico needs to increase its manufacturing capacity in order to boost employment and reduce the burden of imports. The resulting demand for capital goods for industry has led to trading deficits. Home industries are providing increased exports, and it is possible that the deficit will be eliminated within a few years. The country's large oil reserves give Mexico a high credit rating in the world's money markets. Very large international loans have financed the major exporting and primary activities.

Inflation has been a serious problem. Having risen to an annual rate of 27% at the end of 1976, it was running at 16.8% over 1978. The United States remains by far the most important of Mexico's trading partners with about 60% of overseas trade in 1976, though its share is decreasing.

Agriculture is lagging behind the rest of productive industry, but is now beginning to show the benefits of higher prices for its steadily increasing exports. The rapid population growth makes continued economic progress essential if a high level of unemployment is to be avoided.

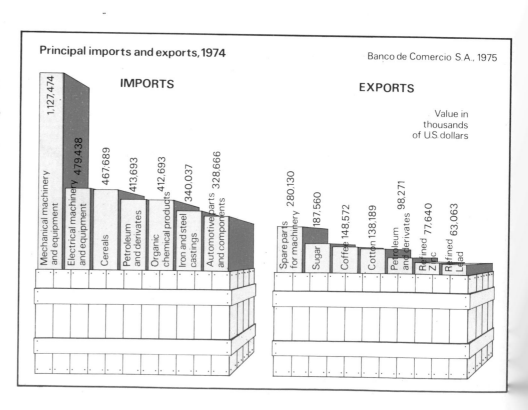

Principal imports and exports, 1974 — Banco de Comercio S.A., 1975

Employment and Productivity

Mexico is evolving rapidly towards a more diversified economy, and each year the manufacturing industries have a greater share of the GNP.

The large agricultural work force has been declining with the drift of labour to the industrial zones. But more intensive and mechanized farming, aided by vast irrigation projects, is now pushing up production per man and per acre. This improvement should especially benefit the heavily populated tropical Gulf country.

Consumption of fish in Mexico has been low in relation to the long coastline and rich fishing grounds. Modern refrigeration and processing plants should give new impetus to the industry, with more jobs and increased exports.

Petrochemicals have become a dynamic industry with great potential for new products and exports.

Mining has been fairly stagnant for some years but modern techniques offer possibilities of a revival in this traditional industry.

Public services and transportation are all being increased and modernised to keep pace with the nation's progress.

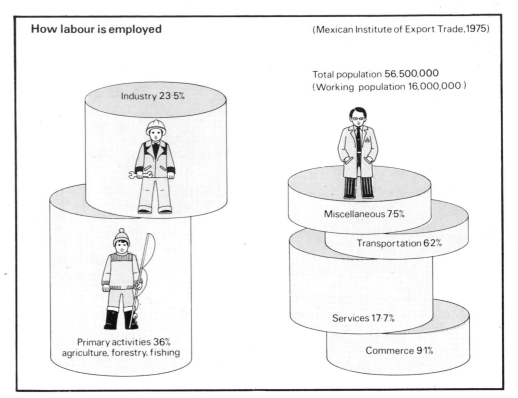

How labour is employed

(Mexican Institute of Export Trade, 1975)

Total population 56,500,000
(Working population 16,000,000)

Industry 23·5%

Primary activities 36%
agriculture, forestry, fishing

Miscellaneous 7·5%

Transportation 6·2%

Services 17·7%

Commerce 9·1%

Agriculture in Mexico

Wheat
Maize
Barley
Rice
Citrus Fruits
Grapes
Coffee
Cocoa
Sugar Cane
Groundnuts
Bananas
Sisal & Henequen
Cotton
Tobacco
Cattle
Pigs
Sheep
Principal Fishing Areas

Agriculture in Mexico

The development of agriculture, despite its decreased share of the Gross National Product in recent years has made remarkable progress. Production has more than tripled.

Successful agriculture under Mexican conditions depends to a great extent on irrigation. The Government's policies have been directed, therefore, to more efficient use of the country's water resources. Nearly a thousand dams have been built.

Of Mexico's total area, approximately 77% lies in arid zones. It is estimated that only 15.2% of Mexico is suitable for agricultural cultivation. 81·3% of the potentially tillable land depends upon seasonal rains, 15% is irrigated, and only 3.7% is humid, with a year round rainfall.

Technical aid and farm credits have changed Mexico from a producer of a single major crop (maize) into a country which grows a great variety of important crops. These crops in general meet domestic demands and provide surpluses for export. Sugar cane, beans, maize, cotton, coffee, sorghum, wheat, alfalfa, rice, citrus fruits and tropical fruits are grown. Maize and beans still form the staple diet of many Mexicans.

Special encouragement is being given to stock raising, forestry, and fruit growing, and a very substantial expansion of sugar production is being planned jointly with Cuba.

Domestic food production has not kept up with the increase in population. Between 1970 and 1975 supplies increased at an average 1.7% per year, while the population grew by 3.5% per year. Periodic water shortages make the problem worse.

59

Gazetteer

Acapulco (17 0N 99 57W). Mexico's largest and most popular international tourist resort, on Pacific coast. Tropical climate, splendid beaches, superb sea fishing and aquatic sports. Pop. 150,000.

Aguascalientes (22 0N 102 12W). Colonial city, State capital, and spa centre. Famous gardens and catacombs. Extensive vineyards and mining areas. Pop. 250,000.

Baja California (28 0N 113 30W). A 1,223 km. (760 miles) long peninsula stretching southwards from U.S. California border. Mostly arid mountains and desert country, sparsely populated except at fringes. Fishing and tourism rapidly developing.

Campeche (19 50N 90 30W). Ancient and beautiful Colonial port and State capital, protected by massive fortress walls. Violent buccaneering history. Leading shrimp fishing centre. Pop. 60,000.

Chichén Itzá (19 50N 88 28W). World famous archaeological zone in Yucatan. Founded about 450 A.D. and occupied by Toltecs and Mayas. Magnificent temples superbly restored, notably those of Castillo, Warriors, and Nuns. Good hotels.

Chihuahua (28 47N 106 20W). Capital of its State and a mining centre surrounded by vast cattle ranches. Home of Revolutionary hero, Pancho Villa, and breed of miniature dogs. Pop. 320,000.

Ciudad Juárez (31 40N 106 28W). Mexico's largest border city, founded 1662. Extensive tourist facilities, shops, markets, bullrings, nightclubs. Pop. 350,000.

Cuernavaca (18 50N 99 20W). Attractive Colonial capital of Morelos State. Warm, equable climate favoured by many foreign residents. Cortés Palace (1530) contains Diego Rivera frescoes. Franciscan cathedral begun 1529. Very beautiful Borda Gardens. Pop. 65,000.

Durango (24 12N 105 15W). Capital of its State, handsome old Colonial mining town noted for its dry, sunny climate. Many John Wayne western films made here. Pop. 150,000.

Guadalajara (20 40N 103 17W). Second largest city in Mexico, capital of Jalisco State. Beautiful Colonial centre, founded in 1537, surrounded by fast-growing modern suburbs. Curiously styled, massive cathedral. Oldest church is San Francisco, built 1550. Famous for native handicrafts, music and regional dances, colourful markets, rodeos, and animated street life. Pop. 1,750,000.

Guanajuato (21 10N 101 0W). Capital of its State, and one of the most beautiful old silver mining towns in Mexico. Built on mountain slopes, has many splendid churches and palaces in its narrow, cobbled streets. La Valenciana silver mine was the world's richest for centuries. Pop. 60,000.

Mazatlán (23 20N 106 20W). Leading commercial and fishing port on Pacific coast. Extensive shrimp processing factories. Ferry service to Baja California. Game fishing and sailing centre. Pop. 125,000.

Mérida (20 55N 89 40W). A Spanish-Mayan city founded 1542 on pre-Conquest Indian town. The centre of Mexico's most extensive and interesting archaeological area. Clean, dazzling white tropical town of Colonial churches, palaces, and windmills. Outstanding cooking and handicrafts. Henequen plantations are a principal source of hemp. Pop. 285,000.

Mexico City (19 25N 99 5W). One of the world's greatest and fastest-growing capitals. Aztec ruins, Spanish Colonial monuments, contrast with brilliantly designed modern architecture. Emperor Moctezuma's palace once stood on the Zócalo, a huge main square now dominated by Cathedral and National Palace built by Cortés. Pop. 9,000,000.

Monterrey (25 42N 100 22W). A great industrial and steelmaking centre and tourist attraction, founded 1596. Capital of Nuevo León State. Cuauhtémoc brewery is largest in Mexico. Fine shops and markets. Pop. 1,500,000.

Morelia (19 48N 101 0W). Beautiful and elegant Colonial city and State capital. Splendid baroque cathedral, many old churches, convents, and aristocratic palaces. Second oldest university in the Americas founded 1540. A leading centre of handicrafts and folk arts, including superb lacquerware. Pop. 170,000.

Oaxaca (17 15N 96 38W). (Pronounced Wah-HAH-Kah). Delightful Colonial city and State capital in beautiful mountain valley. Santo Domingo church (1575) celebrated for sumptuous interior decoration. Important archaeological sites of Mitla and Monte Albán nearby. Magnificent museum of fabulous archaeological treasures. Pop. 100,000.

Orizaba (19 3N 97 16W). Majestic, snow-capped Pico de Orizaba volcano in Veracruz State is highest point in Mexico (5,700m.). Sacred to the Indians, who call it Citlaltépetl —"Mountain of the Star". Colonial city of Orizaba nearby, with cotton mills and famous brewery. Pop. 100,000.

Pachuca (20 13N 98 45W). Capital of Hidalgo State, is largest silver mining centre of Mexico. Many mines have been in continuous operation for hundreds of years, notably Real del Monte. A colony of Cornish miners settled here and their pasties are still popular. Pop. 85,000.

Palenque (17 34N 91 58W). Mayan archaeological site of outstanding importance in Chiapas State. Dramatic setting on hilltop, in tropical rain forest, for palace and temples with superb stucco carving, and unique tomb discovered in pyramid. Has been described as the Angkor Wat of the Americas.

Pátzcuaro (19 30N 101 40W). An ancient Tarascan Indian market town near a beautiful lake of the same name in Michoacán State. Famous centre for handicrafts and folk arts, with outstanding good shops and markets. Pop. 30,000.

Popocatépetl (18 45N 99 40W). The "Smoking Mountain" is the higher at 5,452m. of the two snow capped volcanoes dominating the Valley of Mexico. The other is Ixtaccíhuatl—"The White Woman"—so called because of the shape of its crests, reaching a height of 5,214m.

Puebla (19 11N 98 15W). A completely Spanish looking city, capital of its State, famous for Talavera tiles and onyx, both extensively used in many Colonial churches and palaces. Casa Alfeñique—"Gingerbread House"—remarkable example of Puebla architecture. Pop. 500,000.

Querétaro (20 47N 100 12W). Capital of its State and one of the most historic cities of Mexico. Magnificent churches, splendid palaces, and beautiful plazas abound. Struggle for Independence plotted here. Emperor Maximilian executed 1867. Mexican Constitution signed 1917. Pop. 110,000.

San Cristobal de las Casas (17 14N 92 32W). Wonderfully preserved old Spanish town in cool mountain country in Chiapas State. Picturesquely dressed Indians throng cobbled streets on market days. Named after its first Bishop, Bartolomé de las Casas, who staunchly protected the Indians in early Conquest days. Pop. 35,000.

San Miguel de Allende (20 54N 100 44W). Founded 1542 in Guanajuato State. Many notable churches and mansions line cobbled streets. Large foreign colony of artists and writers. Birthplace of Ignacio Allende, the Independence hero. Favourite shopping centre for tinware and textiles. Pop. 40,000.

Tampico (22 20N 98 12W). Oil centre and important Gulf port on Panuco River. Founded by Cortés in 1523 but is a wholly modern and dynamic city with extensive docks and oil refineries. Pop. 200,000.

Taxco (18 34N 99 37W). Picturesque little colonial town founded 1528 in Guerrero State. Silver mines ensured great prosperity. Many beautiful buildings, notably the magnificent Santa Prisca church. The whole town has been declared a national monument. Famous naturalist Baron Von Humboldt lived here. Very fine local craftsmanship in silver and gemstones. Pop. 25,000.

Tijuana (32 30N 117 30W). Baja California border city near American San Diego naval base. Originally El Rancho de Tia Juana—"Aunt Jane's Ranch". A large, modern city designed for tourists' pleasures and shopping. Pop. 225,000.

Toluca (19 25N 99 37W). Capital of State of Mexico, at 2,638m. altitude; is often a chilly place. Many austere Colonial buildings. Famous for its vast Friday market attended by thousands of Indians from nearby villages. The 4,505m. high volcano, Nevado de Toluca, looms over the city. Pop. 240,000.

Vera Cruz (19 13N 96 18W). Named "Town of the True Cross" by Cortés on landing there 1519. Mexico's premier seaport and metropolis of the richest State in the country. Animated, cosmopolitan, busy modern city famous for its seafood restaurants and lovely music and dancing. Pop. 325,000.

Index

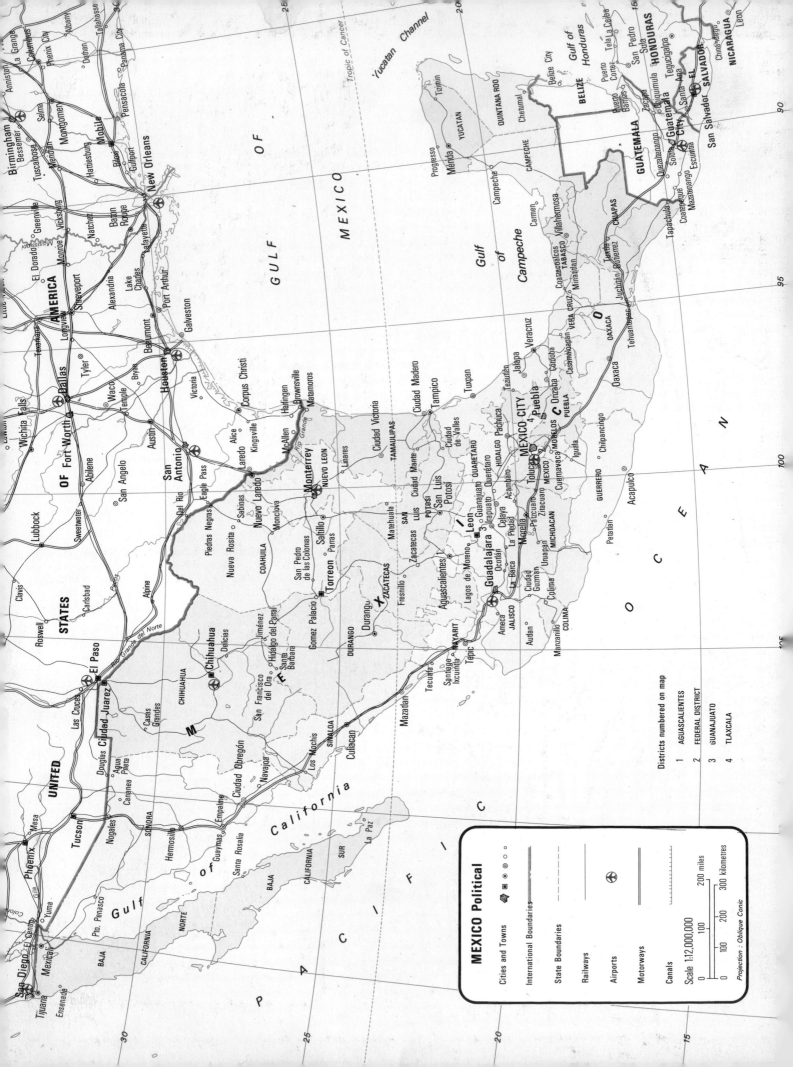